DIALOGUE WITH CARL ROGERS

DIALOGUES IN CONTEMPORARY PSYCHOLOGY SERIES

Richard I. Evans, Series Editor

DIALOGUE WITH **GORDON ALLPORT**
DIALOGUE WITH **ERIK ERIKSON**
DIALOGUE WITH **ERICH FROMM**
DIALOGUE WITH **C.G. JUNG**
DIALOGUE WITH **R.D. LAING**
DIALOGUE WITH **JEAN PIAGET**
DIALOGUE WITH **CARL ROGERS**
DIALOGUE WITH **B.F. SKINNER**
PSYCHOLOGY AND **ARTHUR MILLER**

DIALOGUE WITH CARL ROGERS

Richard I. Evans

PRAEGER

PRAEGER SPECIAL STUDIES • PRAEGER SCIENTIFIC

Library of Congress Cataloging in Publication Data

Evans, Richard Isadore, 1922-
Dialogue with Carl Rogers.

(Dialogues in contemporary psychology series)
Reprint. Originally published: Carl Rogers.
1st ed. New York : Dutton, 1975.
Bibliography: p.
Includes index.
1. Rogers, Carl Ransom, 1902-
2. Psychologists—United States—Biography. 3. Client-centered psychotherapy. I. Title. II. Series: Evans, Richard Isadore, 1922- . Dialogues with notable contributors to personality theory.
BF109.R63E9 1981 150.19′5′0924 81-15373
ISBN 0-03-059929-6 AACR2

Pages xliv—l reprinted by permission of the American Association for the Advancement of Science from *Science,* Vol. 124, Nov. 30, 1956. Pages 119-147 reprinted by permission of the American Psychological Association from *American Psychologist,* Vol. 29, No. 2, February 1974.

Published in 1981 by Praeger Publishers
CBS Educational and Professional Publishing
a Division of CBS Inc.
521 Fifth Avenue, New York, New York 10175 U.S.A.

123456789 145 987654321
Printed in the United States of America

*To my lovely wife
and children*

Introduction to the Praeger Edition

In the history of contemporary psychology, Carl Rogers represents that rare clinician who never lost sight of the importance of testing postulates in his system, even though his approach received almost instant acclaim among counselors and psychotherapists. That his techniques for dealing with human problems appeared not only to work but were effective with relatively short time frames, did not seduce him into ignoring the need to test the foundations of his approach. With behavior therapy, which had enjoyed a broad advocacy in the current scene, beginning to focus increasingly on the importance of self-management, it appears to be particularly timely to publish a new edition of this book. Carl Rogers, from the very start, emphasized the critical importance of self-management in counseling and psychotherapy. In the dialogue in this book Dr. Rogers is almost prophetic. He anticipates the ultimate limitations of Skinner's behaviorism in its underestimation of self-determinism for influencing the solutions to human problems. Making available this new edition of **DIALOGUE WITH CARL ROGERS** will allow an even greater audience to share the insights of one of the most sophisticated psychological explorers of the self-determinism paradigm.

ACKNOWLEDGMENTS

In the long process involved in filming and taping the dialogues with Carl Rogers and transcribing, editing, and integrating them into the present volume, I am indebted to a great many individuals. Though space prohibits mentioning everyone who so kindly assisted me in this venture, I wish to express my appreciation to at least some of them.

Grateful acknowledgment is made to the University of Houston for permission to utilize the printed texts of the filmed and taped dialogue. Mr. James Bauer of the University of Houston functioned in the demanding role of technical director for the taping and filming sessions and should be mentioned among those who have greatly assisted me. Thanks also to Ms. Bettye Raines for her editorial suggestions, collating, and thoughtfulness in typing the final manuscript in the face of a tight deadline.

I am grateful for the support of the National Science Foundation, without which this project could not have been implemented.

Thanks are accorded to Dr. Richard Farson, Director of the Esalen Institute, for his provocative introduction to *Carl Rogers: The Man and His Ideas.*

We appreciate Dr. Rogers' willingness to allow us to reproduce three (one original) of his earlier papers (and B. F. Skinner's for reproducing his joint paper with Dr. Rogers, "Some Issues Concerning the Control of Human Behavior") and we are grateful to publishers, which include: *Science* for "Some Issues Concerning the Control of Human Behavior" and *The American Psychologist* for "In Retrospect–Forty-six Years."

Thanks are accorded graduate student Nancy Ann Potter, who made valuable contributions both editorially and in checking relevant bibliographical sources as well as assisting in collating the final form of the manuscript.

Finally, the wonderful cooperation of Carl Rogers cannot be emphasized enough. Not only was he willing to participate in the filming and audio-taping sessions involved in this project, but his genuine kindness and good humor during the course of these sessions contributed to a most pleasant atmosphere.

Richard I. Evans
Professor of Psychology
University of Houston

CONTENTS

INTRODUCTION

Part A—*Some Perspective on the Dialogue Style and Content*

The present book constitutes the eighth in a series based on dialogues with some of the world's outstanding contributors to psychology. To avoid possible misunderstanding of the goals of the dialogue style used in this volume, some perspective may be of value. Designed hopefully as an innovative teaching device, the series was launched in 1957 with completion of dialogues with the late Carl Jung and Ernest Jones, supported by a grant from the Fund for the Advancement of Education. The series is being continued under a current grant from the National Science Foundation. A basic purpose of the project is to produce for teaching purposes a series of films that introduce the viewer to outstanding contributors to the field of psychology and human behavior. We hope that these films may also serve as documents of increasing value to the history of the behavioral sciences.*

The books in this series are based on edited transcripts of the dialogue, including audiotaped discussions as well as the contents of the films. These dialogues are designed to introduce the reader to the contributor's major ideas and points of view, conveying through the extemporaneousness of the dialogue style a feeling for the personality of the contributor.

When we completed the first book in the series based on dialogues with Jung and Jones (Evans, 1964), we thought the word *conversation* could best be used in the title to describe the process and content. We soon discovered that this implied to potential readers something a bit more casual and superficial than we had intended. Even though we emphasize spontaneity in the dialogues with our participants, this should not detract from the significance of the content. We would hope that a relatively informal discussion with an outstanding contributor to a discipline, as he seriously examines his own work, will not be less significant by virtue of its informality than more formal presentations. A more detailed description of the philosophy and techniques of this project is reported elsewhere (Evans, 1969c). However, a few points bearing on the content of these volumes can be emphasized here. Since the questions are intended to reflect many of the published writings of the interviewee, it might be expected that a comprehensive summary of his work is evoked. The selec-

* The films are distributed by Macmillan Films, Inc., 34 MacQuesten Parkway, South, Mt. Vernon, New York 10550.

tivity necessary in developing the questions within a limited time interval does not always provide the basis for an inclusive summary. In fact, we are hoping to present a teaching technique leading away from the trend observed among many of our students today —to become increasingly content with only secondary sources to gain information concerning our major contributors in the various disciplines. The material—films and books—resulting from our dialogues provides a novel "original source" exposure to the ideas of outstanding persons, which, in turn, may stimulate the viewer or reader to go back to the original writings, which develop more fully the ideas presented through our "dialogue."

The term *dialogue* was finally adopted instead of *conversation* to describe our content and method, implying a more programmed approach. The interpretation of the term *dialogue,* however, also implies a "challenge" or a confrontation with the individual being "interviewed." To some, the term suggests that the questioner is using the individual being questioned as a tool to project the questioner's teaching role in the situation. My goals here would preclude either of these interpretations. It is my intention that these dialogues reflect a constructive, novel method of teaching, with my role as interviewer being neither the center of focus nor the critical challenger. The purpose of this book will be realized if I am perceived as providing a medium through which our distinguished interviewees can express their views. It is within the spirit of these teaching aims that our contributors so generously participate. This has been evident from the very beginning of the project, for example, in a letter from the late Carl Jung, reproduced in the first chapter of *Conversations with Carl Jung and Reactions from Ernest Jones* (Evans, 1964). The use of such sessions primarily as a background for critical examination of the views of the participants must be left to another type of project, since even if this "critical set" were to be emphasized in my questioning, it might be difficult to introduce the reader to the contributor's views and to criticize them as well, within the limited time commitment. I expect that some of the participants who agreed to work with us on this project would not have done so if they had sensed primarily a critical attack on their work.

As was the case with subjects of the earlier books in the series, Carl Jung and Ernest Jones (Evans, 1964), Erich Fromm (Evans, 1966), Erik Erikson (Evans, 1969a), B. F. Skinner (Evans, 1968), Arthur Miller (Evans, 1969b), Gordon Allport[1] (Evans, 1971), and Jean Piaget (Evans, 1973), it is hoped that the dialogue presentation allows the reader to be introduced to, or to reexamine, some of Carl Rogers' ideas through a relatively extemporaneous situation. It should be pointed out, however, that in his writings, as Rogers expresses himself in his own unique style, he has the opportunity to rewrite and polish until he deems the finished product satisfactory. In the spontaneity of our discussion, he is called upon to develop his ideas extemporaneously. I hope that this element of spon-

[1] We were very pleased when *Gordon Allport: The Man and His Ideas* was honored by receiving the 1971 American Psychological Foundation Media Award in the book category.

taneity may present more of the "man behind the book" while losing none of the ideas central to his thought.

Because preservation of this naturalness of communication is essential to the purposes of each volume in this series, few liberties have been taken with the basic content of Dr. Rogers' responses to my questions, although some editorial license had to be exercised to shift effectively from oral to printed communication in the service of accuracy, readability, clarity, and grammatical construction. So the dialogue presented here duplicates insofar as possible the tenor of the exchange between Dr. Rogers and myself as it actually took place. In spite of the editing that was necessary, it was a pleasant surprise to review our hours of discussion and to realize how few deletions and alterations were required. We hope that this dialogue makes available to the reader some reactions not readily obtainable from Rogers' more traditional didactic presentations or from the secondary sources on his work in the literature.

Rather than attempt to summarize all of the major concepts presented in the dialogue as we did in some of the previous volumes in this series, I shall again—as I did in the Fromm, Skinner, and Erikson volumes—take the liberty of briefly presenting frameworks that I find valuable in teaching personality theory to students, hoping they may, in turn, be of value to the reader of this book in comprehending the backdrop against which we may look at contemporary contributors to psychology such as Carl Rogers. Since, when Carl Rogers came on the scene, personality and psychotherapy were dominated by the influence of psychoanalytical theory, the evolution of psychoanalysis from traditional Freud to the so-called neo-Freudians figures prominently in the Rogers dialogue as a point of departure and will be amplified in the discussion that follows.

There are three frameworks around which I believe current approaches to personality psychology can be analyzed in order to help to locate any theoretical position within the matrix of general personality theory. These frameworks are really descriptive approaches to the understanding of personality that develop theoretically from basic orientations focusing around the unconscious-oriented biological determinism, social environment-oriented cultural determinism, or experience-oriented self-determinism.

One group of contributors, emphasizing unconscious-oriented biological determinism, has been considered more or less traditionally psychoanalytical. It includes such writers as Hans Sachs and Ernest Jones, as well as Freud himself. This group has been characterized as emphasizing what Freud called "repetition compulsion," a concept that maintains that the first five years of life, which are strongly influenced by biological propensities, are very important in human development because they set the stage for and determine a life-style that is manifested continuously throughout the individual's lifetime; central to this postulate is the notion of the Oedipal complex. Another important aspect of traditional Freudian theory was brought out by Ernest Jones in our dialogue with him (Evans,

1964), in which he unabashedly makes the statement, "Well, man is, after all, an animal." Some people think that this is a cynical view, although Jones denied that Freud was inordinately cynical. Interestingly, the increasing impact of ethology on contemporary psychology, which will be discussed in a forthcoming volume dealing with Konrad Lorenz (Evans, in press), has reopened this issue in a new and somewhat more palatable-to-psychologists vein. Freud's earliest picture of man is that of an organism dominated to a large degree by its id—the animal, biological side of him—against which the ego—the conscious, the self of man—is fighting a tough battle. He is seen as just barely able to hold his head above water in the struggle to keep from being drowned by the animal he basically is. This view of man, as articulated in Freud's early works, was also accepted by many of the early followers of Freud. With Freud, they believed that the center of man's motivation and energy is the sexual libido, which to them was a manifestation of the dominant animal aspect of man. Although Freud in his later work began to emphasize other aspects of man's makeup also, many thinkers continue to perceive the classical psychoanalytical position in terms of early views of Freud. Actually, the above description is probably a vast oversimplification of Freud's view, as Fromm (Evans, 1966) and Erikson (Evans, 1969a), for example, have implied.

Another group of contributors, the neo-Freudians, has placed more stress on the effects of social-environmental-cultural influences on man's development. To the neo-Freudians, the early Freudians would appear to have taken too seriously the notion that the instinctual animal nature, the repetition compulsion, and a general biological patterning of early development are found *universally,* and that these elements dominate man's nature. This, too, has been more recently underlined by ethologists. The neo-Freudians take exception to this concept of universality. They believe that man is primarily a product of the specific kind of culture in which he lives, and that learning plays a much more important part than does biological patterning in the development of personality.

The late Karen Horney, for example, a prominent neo-Freudian who had been with the Berlin Psychoanalytic Institute, became so disturbed by many notions in the biological orientation of the early Freudian position, such as the postulation of male superiority evidenced by the assertion that penis envy was intrinsically characteristic of women, that she broke away from the orthodox Freudian position. She developed a view (e.g. Horney, 1937) that man is shaped to a significant extent by the society with which he must cope when he deals with the anxieties of reality. She considered this anxiety produced by societal pressures more important in shaping man than his anxiety about overcoming his basic biological animal nature.

Again, as indicated in one of our earlier volumes (Evans, 1966), although Fromm does not like the label neo-Freudian, he too certainly takes exception to Freud's emphasis on the Oedipal situation so central to Freud's "biological unfolding" view of man's development.

Virtually all contemporary American psychologists have attempted to place man within his social milieu, in the belief that it constitutes the essential force in shaping personality. The neo-Freudians, however, still did not pay adequate attention to the principles of learning that are necessary to account for the shaping influence of the social environment. B. F. Skinner (Evans, 1968), moving away from a focus on "personality" to a focus on behavior, supplied a cogent model of the process of shaping behavior, which was already in the Zeitgeist when Carl Rogers was formulating his early views of conceptualization. Rogers began to see this as a threat (see the Rogers-Skinner debate which follows this essay) in the sense that Skinner's principles involved control of the individual. Rogers, unlike the Freudians, however, did formalize a set of learning principles that he believed could be useful but not controlling. So, the neo-Freudian group (e.g. Kardiner, 1939; Sullivan, 1953) challenged psychoanalysis to extend the study of man at least beyond Freud's early basic tenets, but still lacked a sufficient base in learning principles.

Another characteristic of the neo-Freudian group is evident in their techniques of psychotherapy. The traditional Freudians considered psychotherapy a five-day-a-week affair that takes from three to five years of intensive therapy before it can be successful; the neo-Freudians, like Carl Rogers, believed that situational factors were much more important, and claimed to have achieved results with much shorter periods of psychotherapy.

Somewhere between the neo-Freudians and the traditional Freudians there is a group of three significant individuals whom we might describe as Freudian dissentients; for although each of them worked closely with Freud, each subsequently broke with him or was repudiated by him for one reason or another. Carl Jung, Otto Rank, and Alfred Adler would be included in this group.

Adler's early work (e.g., 1927) placed the primary emphasis on the social man, and it might be said that Adler set the stage for the emergence of the neo-Freudian group. In a different direction, although many of his ideas about early biological conceptions were in agreement with Freud's, Rank's preoccupation with the "will" and its development of autonomy introduced a type of self-determinism that Freud did not emphasize. Interestingly enough, Rank had a marked influence on Carl Rogers.

As became apparent in our dialogue, Carl Jung (Evans, 1964) had moved away from Freud's basic tenets, while retaining Freud's idea of the unconscious, expanding it into a race and an individual unconscious. He incorporated into the race unconscious Freud's early notion of archetypes, developing this concept beyond Freud's postulation. However, with his central conception of individuation (much like Rogers' "growth principle"), Jung also moved away from the emphasis on biological determinism. Jung, perhaps more profoundly than either Adler or Rank, turned toward the idea of the development of an ultimately self-determined spiritual being that transcends the biological forces acting on man. This led him to consider many metaphysical conceptions, obviously not in keeping with present-day notions of a scientific psychology.

A great deal of thought today continues to reflect the greater concern for man's individuality and self-responsibility than is found in either biological or cultural determinism. Of course, Carl Rogers is in the forefront of this movement. Also central to this position are the works of Abraham Maslow (1954), Rollo May (1961), the distinguished philosophical theologian Paul Tillich (1952), and the philosophers Edmund Husserl (1952) and Martin Heidegger (1959). Also, many more theoretically oriented psychologists such as Gordon Allport (Evans, 1971) and Harold G. McCurdy (1953) reflect an increased concern with the autonomy of the self.

However, in any theoretical discussion of "determinism" and personality theory, the behavioristic orientation may still be the most significant theoretical reference group for American academic and research psychologists. As the leading contemporary exponent of this view, B. F. Skinner interprets not merely cultural influences in a broad sense, but the immediate environment in a narrow sense as being the significant shaping force on the individual. As environment is experimentally controlled to modify behavior (even in the clinical situation), very few asumptions concerning the "internal workings" of personality have to be made. So the Skinner-Rogers "debates" from the beginning dealt with the crucial philosophical and theoretical issues raised by the "determinism" issue.

At various points in the dialogue, Dr. Rogers was given an opportunity to deal directly or indirectly with the differences among the three positions represented by the biological, cultural, and self-deterministic points of view. He feels that in his approach he has not ignored these conceptualizations. However, to him, generic bases of behavior vis-à-vis biological, social, or self-deterministic constructs are less important than focusing on the *synthesis* of the individual's self, which is, among other things, an actor in society.

Another area in the dialogue relates to the fact that only within recent years have many psychologists come to recognize the need to involve themselves with the issues of immediate concern to society. Much of psychology might appear to the outsider to be for the exclusive benefit of psychologists. On the current scene, Carl Rogers has been in the forefront in broadening the goals of psychology (e.g. Sanford, 1965; Evans, 1966a), including a greater concern with human problems within the province of psychology. His efforts appear to provide provocative base lines for such endeavors, within a restrained and professionally acceptable framework.

It must be said that, aside from anything else he does, Carl Rogers must be regarded as a significant contributor not only to psychology as a discipline but also as a respondent to society's greatest challenge—the need to develop a means for the improvement of the intellectual and psychological health of its members and, by so doing, to develop an optimistic, self-determined, positive philosophy about human existence rather than one that is cynical, negative, and externally determined.

To expand the reader's knowledge of Rogers and

his philosophy beyond what appears in the dialogue, two previously published papers and two new papers are included. One part of the introduction includes a paper by Dr. Richard Farson, director of the Esalen Institute. This paper, "Carl Rogers, Quiet Revolutionary," was prepared by Farson for the journal *Education* in honor of the selection of Rogers as one of the "Gold Medal Educators of the 70's." Another paper included in the introduction, as mentioned earlier, is one of the early and, many believe, still most cogent of the "debates" between Carl Rogers and B. F. Skinner on the control of behavior. Finally, in the back of the book are two papers by Dr. Rogers. One was delivered on the occasion of his being awarded the Distinguished Professional Contribution award at the 1973 American Psychological Association meeting. The other is an original statement of his assessment of the present state of society and his hopes for the future.

If the reader is encouraged to pursue the work of Carl Rogers in greater depth, a relatively complete bibliography of his writings is provided, in addition to the references noted in this book.

Part B—*Carl Rogers, Quiet Revolutionary*

Richard Farson
Director, Esalen Institute, San Francisco

Carl Rogers is not known for his politics. People are more likely to associate his name with widely acclaimed innovations in counseling technique, personality theory, philosophy of science, psychotherapy research, encounter groups, student-centered teaching; his thoughts on human nature, his descriptions of the person of the future, his views on marriage and coupling, etc.—each one a stunning contribution by itself. But in recent years, viewing the body of his work as a whole, I have come to think of him more as a political figure, a man whose cumulative effect on society has made him one of the most important social revolutionaries of our time.

I would like to explain that statement by beginning with a quote from Rogers' autobiography. It describes a point at which he made the discovery that was to change not only his way of thinking about human relationships but just about everyone else's, too.

> I had been working with a highly intelligent mother whose boy was something of a hellion. The problem was clearly her early rejection of the boy, but over many interviews I could not help her to this insight. I drew her out, I gently pulled together the evidence she had given, trying to help her see the pattern.
>
> But we got nowhere. Finally I gave up. I told her that it seemed we had both tried but we had failed and that we might as well give up our contacts. She agreed. So we concluded the interview, shook hands, and she walked to the door of the office.
>
> Then she turned and asked, "Do you ever take adults for counseling here?" When I replied in the affirmative, she said, "Well, then, I would like some help." She came back to the chair she had just left and began to pour out her despair about her marriage, her troubled relationship with her husband, her sense of failure and confusion, all very different from the sterile "case history" she had given before. Real therapy began then and ultimately it was highly successful—for her and for her son.
>
> This incident was one of a number which helped me to experience the fact—only fully realized later—that it is the *client* who knows what hurts, what directions to go, what problems are crucial, what experiences have been deeply buried. It began to occur to me that unless I had a need to demonstrate my own cleverness and learning, I would do better to rely upon the client for the direction of movement in the process.

What a simple, obvious, marvelous, powerful, revolutionary idea. An idea that is now so much a part of our understanding not only of therapy but of every field of human endeavor that we have all but forgotten where it came from.

It is Rogers' style to let go of ideas, to share them, to avoid ownership, to prevent them from becoming dogmatized and identified solely with him. By his having let go of them they have developed lives of their own and, as a result, have pervaded all human affairs. Many of those who practice his approach or have adopted his philosophy do not think of themselves as Rogerian. Some have probably never heard of him.

With that simple idea he empowered hundreds of thousands of professionals and laymen, who would otherwise never have seen themselves as personal counselors, to engage in genuinely helping relationships. His approach, though not easy to learn, is so elegant in concept and so dramatically rewarding in practice that it swept not only psychology but almost every other profession as well.

Rogers has always been a bit puzzled that he is taken more seriously in other fields than he is in his own field of psychology. Professionals from education, religion, nursing, medicine, psychiatry, law, business, government, public health, law enforcement, race relations, social work—the list goes on and on—all came to feel that here, finally, was an approach which enabled them to succeed on the previously neglected human dimensions of their jobs, to reach the people for whom they felt responsible but were often unable to help.

Rogers showed how the conditions for a therapeutic relationship could be generated by people who may not have had "proper" training. His research demonstrated that these conditions were neither mysterious nor dependent upon formal professional experience, and might in fact be present in anyone. Rogers described them this way:

> . . . constructive personality growth and change comes about only when the client perceives and experiences a certain psychological climate in the relationship. The conditions which constitute this climate do not consist of knowledge, intellectual training, orientation in some school of thought, or techniques. They are feelings or attitudes which must be experienced by the counselor and perceived by the client if they are to be effective. Those I have singled out as being essential are: a sensitive empathic understanding of the client's feelings and personal meanings; a warm, acceptant prizing of the client; and an unconditionality in this positive regard.

In effect he managed to *demystify* the practice of therapy. He showed how it really works. And he did this so convincingly and helpfully that thousands were encouraged to try to develop such relationships with their own clients, patients, students, employees, customers, or inmates. His demystification of therapy not only made extensions into other fields possible but it encouraged many other workers to further uncover the mystifying practices of psychotherapists.

Many of those from the political left now practicing various forms of radical therapy owe some debt to Rogers for his pioneering work in making therapeutic processes understandable and therapeutic methods available to any and all who would use them, regardless of the user's academic credentials. In the radical therapists' battle to rid psychiatry of its mystique and bring psychological help to people whom they feel are prevented, mainly for political, economic, or social reasons, from obtaining it, Carl Rogers is an important ally. His early effectiveness in demystifying the psychotherapy professions brought helping relationships to millions who would otherwise have been treated less knowledgeably and less humanely.

During the 1930s, 1940s, and 1950s he was virtually alone in his struggle to keep medicine from gaining a stranglehold on the helping professions. Somehow he knew then what many have come to know now: that no single profession or discipline has a corner on the market of knowledge about human affairs. His lonely battles with medicine, psychiatry, psychoanalysis, and psychoanalytically dominated professions such as psychiatric social work, are largely forgotten. It is difficult, sometimes, to remember the days when even highly trained psychologists could not practice therapy. Armed with impressive research findings and a bold vision, he forced the door open and held it open for all who followed.

It was not accomplished without hurt and humiliation. Once, in the mid-1950s, he described to me his painful attempt to deliver a lecture to the assembled psychiatrists at a mental health conference at Harvard, all the while competing with Karl Menninger, the chairman of the meeting, who sat behind him reading papers, studying timetables, swatting flies, taking great pains to avoid showing Rogers the attention and respect that he was ultimately to gain from this profession.

Great respect, even adulation, did eventually come his way and no one has ever handled success better. One of the strengths I admire most in him is his ability to resist the continuing efforts to make him a guru, an idol, the leader of a movement. He has been asked many times to give his name and his leadership to professional associations that might be formed around the basic concepts he has introduced—associations of client-centered or nondirective therapists, for example—but unlike other major contributors he has always eschewed the leadership role, never endorsed anything bearing his name, never tried to become the leader of a school (although he certainly is), never encouraged the fanatical devotion that could easily have been his, never tried to limit the practice of his methods only to those disciples whom he personally anointed.

His determination to avoid such a role has never wavered. I remember one San Francisco lecture audience of a thousand or more enthusiastic supporters who came to have Rogers lead them on a crusade but heard instead a sober and scholarly report of his work. When I asked him after the lecture why he had chosen to address the group in this way, he said that they seemed to him a bit too eager to be carried away by rhetoric and demagoguery and that it was probably better that they hear this material.

He has not only been able to demystify the profession of psychotherapy in general but his own behavior as a therapist as well. Until Rogers changed the rules of the game, psychotherapists only knew about each other's work from dramatic descriptions after the hour was over, possibly tending to present themselves as being somewhat more brilliant than they actually were. Rogers, on the other hand, is willing to document his work, not from his selective recall but from the verbatim transcripts of the interaction. In 1938, on a wire recorder, he was the first to record a therapeutic hour.

Not only was he the first to audio-record his hours but also the first to film them. For years, when no one else had the courage to show what he or she actually said or did in the development of therapeutic relationships, Rogers turned the camera on himself. He is still doing it. One cannot help but respect a person who will show himself both failing and succeeding when it would be easy to play the game the way others have played it, letting us see only that which makes him look wise and competent.

Rogers' fascination with the way things really are, his willingness to carefully document his own and others' behavior, and his fundamental interest in simply making sense out of things combined in him to produce psychotherapy's first scientific researcher. He became the one to bring science into a field previously regarded as unknowable on any scientific basis—more like art or magic. He insisted, against strong opposition, that the seemingly potent phenomena of personal change could be studied with scientific methods of controlled investigation, that the previously sacred therapeutic hour could be recorded and analyzed without damage.

Almost no one thought it could or should be done. But with these new data he was able to assess, phrase by phrase, even word by word, the therapeutic events which led to defensiveness and those which led to insight and exploration, those which built the relationship and those which hindered it. The results were too much for the opposition. Single-handed, he had opened the field of psychotherapy to scientific scrutiny.

Perhaps more than anyone he made psychology the business of normal people and normal people the business of psychology. Before Rogers, psychology conformed to a medical model, to heal the sick. People were thought of as either disturbed or normal and, if the latter, there was nothing psychology could or should do for them. There was nowhere further for normal people to go in their own personal development.

When Rogers came along, he built a base for what was to become psychology's largest area of interest, the normal person and his or her potential for growth and creativity. Rogers did this through a combination of several ideas. First of all, his personality theory made no assumption of diseased processes, unconscious motivation, or developmental history. It wasn't that he believed that these constructs didn't matter or didn't exist, but that an explanation of personality and behavior is most powerful when understood in ahistorical and interpersonal terms. So while Rogers was not the first person to theorize in these terms, he was the person who had sufficient impact on psychological thinking to make it possible for the field of humanistic psychology to emerge.

Actualizing human potentialities for creativity and growth, regarding the person in the here and now, emphasizing the centrality of the self, and placing significance on experience as well as behavior were the fundamental building blocks of humanistic psychology and Rogers supplied them. In this he was clearly the forerunner of people like Abraham Maslow and Rollo May, who eventually came to carry the banner of humanistic psychology and to focus attention on the idea of self-actualization rather than treatment of the sick.

Rogers saw people as being on an endless growth journey—a journey which is sometimes blocked by negative or incongruent images of oneself, sometimes by inhibiting cultural conditions. Freeing people so that they might accelerate this journey became the great challenge of humanistic psychology. Although he might wince at the term, he is in great measure responsible for what came to be called the human potential movement, and he is surely a major force in the development of more than three hundred growth centers in the United States.

His focusing on the achievement of human potentialities has cut two ways, of course. It has given us a new consciousness of what we might become, of human rights and human needs, and has influenced and improved every part of life—from marriage and childrearing to executive leadership.

But by raising our expectations he has also given us a new level of discontent. The discrepancy between what people are ordinarily *able* to make happen in their relationships and what they have come to believe is *possible* to make happen as a result, say, of reading a book by Carl Rogers is the cause of much disruption in their lives. High-order discontent, which comes from rising expectations, is the reason why many people divorce or quit their jobs. But that, of course, is the inevitable, paradoxical, and sometimes calamitous effect of the experiences we value most—education, art, etc. To the extent that these activities give us a new picture of ourselves and our world, a new vision to work for and hope for, the world becomes both a better place and a more difficult one in which to live. And high-level discontent is the stuff upon which revolutions are built.

It is this sort of paradox with which Rogers has the greatest difficulty. By and large he is unable to recognize either the coexistence of opposites or the enormous complexity of human affairs. His is essentially a linear theory, as opposed to a curvilinear one; maximizing rather than optimizing. His concepts, like most others in humanistic psychology, are based on the idea of "the more the better," as opposed to "there can be too much of a good thing." Rogers would have you believe that the more congruence, the more honesty, the more intimacy, the more closeness, the more empathy, the better. Sounds good, but, as is the case with most linear thinking, it fails in the extreme, and that unfortunately is where it is taken by both Rogers and his students who seem to believe that all human problems from marriage to international negotiation should yield to the application of his principles of human communication. They cannot be solved with these techniques because they are not problems in an ordinary sense but complicated paradoxical dilemmas. It is both impossible and ultimately undesirable to try to deal with them in a linear fashion, as if human experience could be smoothed out, as if we could have peaks without valleys. For a revolutionary, Rogers has paid precious little attention to role, power, status, culture, politics, history, systems, technology, and, perhaps most significantly, the paradoxical quality of human experience. There is a kind of omnipotence and optimism in Rogers' work, a belief that all is possible with the tools of client-centered therapy.

In this connection, he continues to try to justify psychotherapy on its weakest point, that it produces constructive behavior change. It sometimes seems to me a pity that psychotherapy derived from medicine, a field where the benefits are expected to last. If it had developed instead out of a different field, say, for example, theatre, then we would not expect it to work after it was over, but only while it was going on. We have unfortunately burdened psychotherapy with an expectation on which it cannot very often deliver, that it will change behavior. In the process we have missed its great value.

We have expected it to fix people, to reform them. People do not need fixing, they are pretty good the way they are. It it more the situations which victimize them that need fixing, but we will not get to that task if we continue to believe that until we get people straightened out there is no point in trying to make changes in organizations or in society at large.

I, for one, hate to see Rogers bother with such a pragmatic, utilitarian question about therapy as "Does it work?" Everything "works"—all brands of therapy, even the off brands, work. So do all forms of religious conversion. Another way of putting this dilemma is that *nothing* "works." All these endeavors yield similar results. None of them is able to show much permanent change.

Rogers has given us a much more powerful and important idea. He has given us a way to be with one another, an ethical basis for human interaction, guidelines for the important considerations in assessing not just the outcome but the process of a relationship.

Rogers has changed behavior all right, but not in the way he believes. He has changed the way we all think about human relationships, the expectations we have about intimate personal contact, the nature of interpersonal and organizational behavior. Without realizing it he has revolutionized our ideas about human affairs. It is in this process that he has changed individuals by the millions.

It is my thesis that Rogers' greatest contribution has not been in giving us a technique to fix people, but in creating a new form, a new definition of relationship in which people can function more fully and be more self-determining. It is this new form that has had such an impact on every social institution and is to a great extent responsible for the revolution in participation that has dominated the social development of the United States in the last decade.

His work is basic to the restructuring of almost every field of human affairs. Consider some of the areas of influence. His ideas are the main ones used to support efforts toward democratic or participative management in industry. There has probably not been a single organizational development or management training program in twenty-five years which has not been built on his theoretical formulations. His ideas opened the way to student-centered teaching and learning and this philosophy of empowering the student contributed subsequently to the students' rights movement. His ideas cleared away the mystique of professionalism in psychiatry and the helping professions and gave impetus to the development and utilization of lay and paraprofessional resources and to the radical therapy movement. His ideas gave strength to dissident clergy unwilling to accept the hierarchical authority of the church. His ideas emphasized self-direction and personal responsibility in all the fields of health and welfare and helped spawn thousands of self-help groups. His idea that the greatest resource for the solution of any problem is the very population that has the problem has led community organizers, welfare specialists, architects, and city planners to involve citizens from all segments of the community in the decisions which will ultimately affect them. His ideas form the core of the encounter-group experience, an experience in participation which has now been a part of the lives of perhaps as many as ten million Americans. His ideas about child-rearing have led millions of Americans to try to solve the problems of parenting in less power-centered, authority-based ways and have contributed directly to the new concepts of children's rights.

Taken together these developments describe and define the participative mood of America. Rogers becomes responsible along with a handful of other social revolutionaries for the healthy subversion of our blind obedience to authority and for the development of a new sense of trust and confidence in ourselves. We must include Rogers' name, not peripherally but centrally, as we identify the people who set the stage for this revolution of participation.

Surprisingly, Rogers has never thought of himself as a political person, never identified himself with social movements. But his work has had a consistent theme—that people can and should be trusted to direct their own lives. To a slogan which he has probably never used, "Power to the people," Rogers has given real substance and meaning.

Unfortunately, in spite of its proven impact, Rogers' work has been corrupted over the years by practitioners who have discovered the technique but not the philosophy. Rogers showed that marvelous things happened when a person was trusted and accepted, when a person's feelings were dignified and respected, when the person was given a sense of safety and understanding. With amazing sensitivity Rogers could stay right with a person's feelings, whatever they were, through all forms of defensiveness and hostility and fear. He followed every turn, every subtlety, and always let the person set the pace and the direction. And while there were many aimless, plodding hours, there were also many breakthroughs of insight and emotionality. When people were allowed to discuss their deepest feelings, whatever they were, and came to feel loved and accepted in the relationship, then they did indeed go into their feelings intensely and the emotions would run high.

But today's practitioners are impatient. They are not satisfied with such a pedestrian approach. They argue that if it is beneficial for people to talk about their feelings, then perhaps it is good to make sure that they do. To accomplish this all sorts of gimmicks have been invented to elicit the expression of feelings. From there it was a small step to *force* a person to talk about feelings. If there were no feelings to talk about, ways could be found to make sure that there would be feelings to talk about. And if tears accompanying the experienced feelings gave them more validity, then screams or nausea would be even more valid. So it has gone, and in the process Rogers' idea of respect for the person is in danger of disappearing. Authoritarian gimmickry seems irresistibly satisfying, even to humanistic psychologists. Rogers himself is sometimes caught up in this trend. Performance seems to be winning out over safety, aggressiveness over acceptance, emotionality over dignity. The newest forms of treatment to which people are flocking by the thousands are almost neofascist in their willingness to use coercion and threat to evoke feelings which supposedly can then be explored to advantage.

As we become aware of the social and political consequences of these authoritarian movements, I believe they will be replaced by a new insistence on the dignity and worth of the individual and the right to self-determination. I would predict, therefore, that we may see, in the not too distant future, a dramatic resurgence of interest in Rogerian psychology. Not because his methods are more potent or intensive or exciting. They aren't. But because they dignify us as persons. We recognize that Rogers cares most about the quality and integrity of relationships and the protection of human rights. When all the varied approaches are weighed, we will see that his protects people best because it protects them against those of us who think we know what's good for them.

Part C—*Some Issues Concerning the Control of Human Behavior: A Symposium*

Carl R. Rogers and B. F. Skinner

I: Skinner

Science is steadily increasing our power to influence, change, mold —in a word, control—human behavior. It has extended our "understanding" (whatever that may be) so that we deal more successfully with people in nonscientific ways, but it has also identified conditions or variables which can be used to predict and control behavior in a new, and increasingly rigorous, technology. The broad disciplines of government and economics offer examples of this, but there is special cogency in those contributions of anthropology, sociology, and psychology which deal with individual behavior. Carl Rogers has listed some of the achievements to date in a recent paper.[1] Those of his ex-

[1] C. R. Rogers, *Teachers College Record* 57, 316 (1956).

amples which show or imply the control of the single organism are primarily due, as we should expect, to psychology. It is the experimental study of behavior which carries us beyond awkward or inaccessible "principles," "factors," and so on, to variables which can be directly manipulated.

It is also, and for more or less the same reason, the conception of human behavior emerging from an experimental analysis which most directly challenges traditional views. Psychologists themselves often do not seem to be aware of how far they have moved in this direction. But the change is not passing unnoticed by others. Until only recently it was customary to deny the possibility of a rigorous science of human behavior by arguing, either that a lawful science was impossible because man was a free agent, or that merely statistical predictions would always leave room for personal freedom. But those who used to take this line have become most vociferous in expressing their alarm at the way these obstacles are being surmounted.

Now, the control of human behavior has always been unpopular. Any undisguised effort to control usually arouses emotional reactions. We hesitate to admit, even to ourselves, that we are engaged in control, and we may refuse to control, even when this would be helpful, for fear of criticism. Those who have explicitly avowed an interest in control have been roughly treated by history. Machiavelli is the great prototype. As Macaulay said of him, "Out of his surname they coined an epithet for a knave and out of his Christian name a synonym for the devil." There were obvious reasons. The control that Machiavelli analyzed and recommended, like most political control, used techniques that were aversive to the controllee. The threats and punishments of the bully, like those of the government operating on the same plan, are not designed—whatever their success—to endear themselves to those who are controlled. Even when the techniques themselves are not aversive, control is usually exercised for the selfish purposes of the controller and, hence, has indirectly punishing effects upon others.

Man's natural inclination to revolt against selfish control has been exploited to good purpose in what we call the philosophy and literature of democracy. The doctrine of the rights of man has been effective in arousing individuals to concerted action against governmental and religious tyranny. The literature which has had this effect has greatly extended the number of terms in our language which express reactions to the control of men. But the ubiquity and ease of expression of this attitude spells trouble for any science which may give birth to a powerful technology of behavior. Intelligent men and women, dominated by the humanistic philosophy of the past two centuries, cannot view with equanimity what Andrew Hacker has called "the specter of predictable man."[2] Even the statistical or actuarial prediction of human events, such as the number of fatalities to be expected on a holiday weekend, strikes many people as uncanny and evil, while the prediction and control of individual behavior is regarded as little less than the work of the

[2] A. Hacker, *Antioch Rev. 14,* 195 (1954).

devil. I am not so much concerned here with the political or economic consequences for psychology, although research following certain channels may well suffer harmful effects. We ourselves, as intelligent men and women, and as exponents of Western thought, share these attitudes. They have already interfered with the free exercise of a scientific analysis, and their influence threatens to assume more serious proportions.

Three broad areas of human behavior supply good examples. The first of these—*personal control*—may be taken to include person-to-person relationships in the family, among friends, in social and work groups, and in counseling and psychotherapy. Other fields are *education* and *government.* A few examples from each will show how nonscientific preconceptions are affecting our current thinking about human behavior.

PERSONAL CONTROL

People living together in groups come to control one another with a technique which is not inappropriately called "ethical." When an individual behaves in a fashion acceptable to the group, he receives admiration, approval, affection, and many other reinforcements which increase the likelihood that he will continue to behave in that fashion. When his behavior is not acceptable, he is criticized, censured, blamed, or otherwise punished. In the first case the group calls him "good"; in the second, "bad." This practice is so thoroughly ingrained in our culture that we often fail to see that it is a technique of control. Yet we are almost always engaged in such control, even though the reinforcements and punishments are often subtle.

The practice of admiration is an important part of a culture, because behavior, which is otherwise inclined to be weak, can be set up and maintained with its help. The individual is especially likely to be praised, admired, or loved when he acts for the group in the face of great danger, for example, or sacrifices himself or his possessions, or submits to prolonged hardship, or suffers martyrdom. These actions are not admirable in any absolute sense, but they require admiration if they are to be strong. Similarly, we admire people who behave in original or exceptional ways, not because such behavior is itself admirable, but because we do not know how to encourage original or exceptional behavior in any other way. The group acclaims independent, unaided behavior in part because it is easier to reinforce than to help.

As long as this technique of control is misunderstood, we cannot judge correctly an environment in which there is less need for heroism, hardship, or independent action. We are likely to argue that such an environment is itself less admirable or produces less admirable people. In the old days, for example, young scholars often lived in undesirable quarters, ate unappetizing or inadequate food, performed unprofitable tasks for a living or to pay for necessary books and materials or for publication. Older scholars and other members of the group offered compensating reinforcement in the form of approval and admiration for these sacrifices. When the modern graduate student receives a generous scholarship, enjoys good living conditions, and has his research and publication subsidized, the grounds for evaluation seem to be pulled from under us. Such a student no longer *needs* admiration to carry him over a series of obstacles (no matter how much he may need it for other reasons), and, in missing certain familiar objects of admiration, we are likely to conclude that such *conditions* are less admirable. Obstacles to scholarly work may serve as a useful measure of motivation—and we may go wrong unless some substitute is found—but we can scarcely defend a deliberate harassment of the student for this purpose. The productivity of any set of conditions can be evaluated only when we have freed ourselves of the attitudes which have been generated in us as members of an ethical group.

A similar difficulty arises from our use of punishment in the form of censure or blame. The concept of responsibility and the related concepts of foreknowledge and choice are used to justify techniques of control using punishment. Was So-and-So aware of the probable consequences of his action, and was the action deliberate? If so, we are justified in punishing him. But what does this mean? It appears to be a question concerning the efficacy of the contingent relations between behavior and punishing consequences. We punish behavior because it is objectionable to us or the group, but in a minor refinement of rather recent origin we have come to withhold punishment when it cannot be expected to have any effect. If the objectionable consequences of an act were accidental and not likely to occur again, there is no point in punishing. We say that the individual was not "aware of the consequences of his action" or that the consequences were not "intentional." If the action could not have been avoided—if the individual "had no choice"—punishment is also withheld, as it is if the individual is incapable of being changed by punishment because he is of "unsound mind." In all these cases—different as they are—the individual is held "not responsible" and goes unpunished.

Just as we say that it is "not fair" to punish a man for something he could not help doing, so we call it "unfair" when one is rewarded beyond his due or for something he could not help doing. In other words, we also object to wasting *reinforcers* where they are not needed or will do no good. We make the same point with the words *just* and *right*. Thus we have no right to punish the irresponsible, and a man has no right to reinforcers he does not earn or deserve. But concepts of choice, responsibility, justice, and so on provide a most inadequate analysis of efficient reinforcing and punishing contingencies because they carry a heavy semantic cargo of a quite different sort, which obscures any attempt to clarify controlling practices or to improve techniques. In particular, they fail to prepare us for techniques based on other than aversive techniques of control. Most people would object to forcing prisoners to serve as subjects of dangerous medical experiments, but few object when they are induced to serve by the offer of return privileges—even when the reinforcing effect of these privileges has been created by forcible deprivation. In the traditional scheme the right to refuse guarantees the individual against coercion or an unfair bargain. But to what extent *can* a prisoner refuse under such circumstances?

We need not go so far afield to make the point. We can observe our own attitude toward personal freedom in the way we resent any interference with what we want to do. Suppose we want to buy a car of a particular sort. Then we may object, for example, if our wife urges us to buy a less expensive model and to put the difference into a new refrigerator. Or we may resent it if our neighbor questions our need for such a car or our ability to pay for it. We would certainly resent it if it were illegal to buy such a car (remember Prohibition); and if we find we cannot actually afford it, we may resent governmental control of the price through tariffs and taxes. We resent it if we discover that we cannot get the car because the manufacturer is holding the model in deliberately short supply in order to push a model we do not want. In all this we assert our democratic right to buy the car of our choice. We are well prepared to do so and to resent any restriction on our freedom.

But why do we not ask *why* it is the car of our choice and resent the forces which made it so? Perhaps our favorite toy as a child was a car, of a very different model, but nevertheless bearing the name of the car we now want. Perhaps our favorite television program is sponsored by the manufacturer of that car. Perhaps we have seen pictures of many beautiful or prestigeful persons driving it—in pleasant or glamorous places. Perhaps the car has been designed with respect to our motivational patterns: the device on the hood is a phallic symbol; or the horsepower has been stepped up to please our competitive spirit in enabling us to pass other cars swiftly (or, as the advertisements say, "safely"). The concept of freedom that has emerged as part of the cultural practice of our group makes little or no provision for recognizing or dealing with these kinds of control. Concepts like "responsibility" and "rights" are scarcely applicable. We are prepared to deal with coercive measures, but we have no traditional recourse with respect to other measures which in the long run (and especially with the help of science) may be much more powerful and dangerous.

EDUCATION

The techniques of education were once frankly aversive. The teacher was usually older and stronger than his pupils and was able to "make them learn." This meant that they were not actually taught but were surrounded by a threatening world from which they could escape only by learning. Usually they were left to their own resources in discovering how to do so. Claude Coleman has published a grimly amusing reminder of these older practices.[3] He tells of a schoolteacher who published a careful account of his services during fifty-one years of teaching, during which he administered: ". . . 911,527 blows with a cane; 124,010 with a rod; 20,989 with a ruler; 136,715 with

[3] C. Coleman, *Bull. Am. Assoc. Univ. Professors* 39, 457 (1953).

the hand; 10,295 over the mouth; 7,905 boxes on the ear [and]; 1,115,800 slaps on the head. . . ."

Progressive education was a humanitarian effort to substitute positive reinforcement for such aversive measures, but in the search for useful human values in the classroom it has never fully replaced the variables it abandoned. Viewed as a branch of behavioral technology, education remains relatively inefficient. We supplement it, and rationalize it, by admiring the pupil who learns *for himself;* and we often attribute the learning process, or knowledge itself, to something *inside* the individual. We admire behavior which seems to have inner sources. Thus we admire one who *recites* a poem more than one who simply *reads* it. We admire one who *knows* the answer more than one who *knows where to look it up*. We admire the *writer* rather than the *reader*. We admire the arithmetician who can do a problem in his head rather than with a slide rule or calculating machine, or in "original" ways rather than by a strict application of rules. In general we feel that any aid or "crutch"—except those aids to which we are now thoroughly accustomed—reduces the credit due. In Plato's *Phaedrus,* Thamus, the king, attacks the invention of the alphabet on similar grounds! He is afraid "it will produce forgetfulness in the minds of those who learn to use it, because they will not practice their memories. . . ." In other words, he holds it more admirable to remember than to use a memorandum. He also objects that pupils "will read many things without instruction . . . [and] will therefore seem to know many things when they are for the most part ignorant." In the same vein we are, today, sometimes contemptuous of book learning, but, as educators, we can scarcely afford to adopt this view without reservation.

By admiring the student for knowledge and blaming him for ignorance, we escape some of the responsibility of teaching him. We resist any analysis of the educational process which threatens the notion of inner wisdom or questions the contention that the fault of ignorance lies with the student. More powerful techniques, which bring about the same changes in behavior by manipulating *external* variables, are decried as brainwashing or thought control. We are quite unprepared to judge *effective* educational measures. As long as only a few pupils learn much of what is taught, we do not worry about uniformity or regimentation. We do not fear the feeble technique; but we should view with dismay a system under which every student learned everything listed in a syllabus—although such a condition is far from unthinkable. Similarly, we do not fear a system which is so defective that the student must *work* for an education; but we are loath to give credit for anything learned without effort—although this could well be taken as an ideal result—and we flatly refuse to give credit if the student already knows what a school teaches.

A world in which people are wise and good without trying, without "having to be," without "choosing to be," could conceivably be a far better world for everyone. In such a world we should not have to "give anyone credit"—we should not need to admire anyone—for being wise and good. From our present point of view we cannot believe that such a world would be admirable. We do not even permit ourselves to imagine what it would be like.

GOVERNMENT

Government has always been the special field of aversive control. The state is frequently defined in terms of the power to punish, and jurisprudence leans heavily upon the associated notion of personal responsibility. Yet it is becoming increasingly difficult to reconcile current practice and theory with these earlier views. In criminology, for example, there is a strong tendency to drop the notion of responsibility in favor of some such alternative as capacity or controllability. But no matter how strongly the facts, or even practical expedience, support such a change, it is difficult to make the change in a legal system designed on a different plan. When governments resort to other techniques (for example, positive reinforcement), the concept of responsibility is no longer relevant and the theory of government is no longer applicable.

The conflict is illustrated by two decisions of the Supreme Court in the 1930s which dealt with, and disagreed on, the definition of control or coercion.[4] The Agricultural Adjustment Act proposed that the Secretary of Agriculture make "rental or benefit payments" to those farmers who agreed to reduce production. The government agreed that the act would be

[4] P. A. Freund *et al.*, *Constitutional Law Cases and Other Problems*, Vol. 1 (Boston: Little, Brown, 1954), p. 233.

unconstitutional if the farmer had been *compelled* to reduce production but was not, since he was merely *invited* to do so. Justice Roberts[5] expressed the contrary majority view of the court that "The power to confer or withhold unlimited benefits is the power to coerce or destroy." This recognition of positive reinforcement was withdrawn a few years later in another case in which Justice Cardozo[6] wrote "To hold that motive or temptation is equivalent to coercion is to plunge the law in endless difficulties." We may agree with him, without implying that the proposition is therefore wrong. Sooner or later the law must be prepared to deal with all possible techniques of governmental control.

The uneasiness with which we view government (in the broadest possible sense) when it does not use punishment is shown by the reception of my utopian novel, *Walden Two*.[7] This was essentially a proposal to apply a behavioral technology to the construction of a workable, effective, and productive pattern of government. It was greeted with wrathful violence. *Life* magazine called it "a travesty on the good life," and "a menace . . . a triumph of mortmain or the dead hand not envisaged since the days of Sparta . . . a slur upon a name, a corruption of an impulse." Joseph Wood Krutch devoted a substantial part of his book, *The Measure of Man*,[8] to attacking my views and those of the protagonist, Frazier, in the same vein, and

[5] *Ibid.*
[6] *Ibid.*, p. 244.
[7] B. F. Skinner, *Walden Two* (New York: Macmillan, 1948).
[8] J. W. Krutch, *The Measure of Man* (Indianapolis, Ind.: Bobbs-Merrill, 1953).

Morris Viteles has recently criticized the book in a similar manner in *Science*.[9] Perhaps the reaction is best expressed in a quotation from *The Quest for Utopia* by Negley and Patrick:

> Halfway through this contemporary utopia, the reader may feel sure, as we did, that this is a beautifully ironic satire on what has been called "behavioral engineering." The longer one stays in this better world of the psychologist, however, the plainer it becomes that the inspiration is not satiric, but messianic. This is indeed the behaviorally engineered society, and while it was to be expected that sooner or later the principle of psychological conditioning would be made the basis of a serious construction of utopia—Brown anticipated it in *Limanora*—yet not even the effective satire of Huxley is adequate preparation for the shocking horror of the idea when positively presented. Of all the dictatorships espoused by utopists, this is the most profound, and incipient dictators might well find in this utopia a guidebook of political practice.[10]

One would scarcely guess that the authors are talking about a world in which there is food, clothing, and shelter for all, where everyone chooses his own work and works on the average only four hours a day, where music and the arts flourish, where personal relationships develop under the most favorable circumstances, where education prepares every child for the social and intellectual life which lies before him, where—in short—people are truly happy, secure, productive, creative, and forward-looking. What is wrong with it? Only one thing: someone "planned it that

[9] M. Viteles, *Science 122*, 1167 (1955).

[10] G. Negley and J. M. Patrick, *The Quest for Utopia* (New York: Schuman, 1952).

way." If these critics had come upon a society in some remote corner of the world which boasted similar advantages, they would undoubtedly have hailed it as providing a pattern we all might well follow—provided that it was clearly the result of a natural process of cultural evolution. Any evidence that intelligence had been used in arriving at this version of the good life would, in their eyes, be a serious flaw. No matter if the planner of *Walden Two* diverts none of the proceeds of the community to his own use, no matter if he has no current control or is, indeed, unknown to most of the other members of the community (he planned that, too), somewhere back of it all he occupies the position of prime mover. And this, to the child of the democratic tradition, spoils it all.

The dangers inherent in the control of human behavior are very real. The possibility of the misuse of scientific knowledge must always be faced. We cannot escape by denying the power of a science of behavior or arresting its development. It is no help to cling to familiar philosophies of human behavior simply because they are more reassuring. As I have pointed out elsewhere,[11] the new techniques emerging from a science of behavior must be subject to the explicit countercontrol which has already been applied to earlier and cruder forms. Brute force and deception, for example, are now fairly generally suppressed by ethical practices and by explicit governmental and religious agencies. A similar countercontrol of scientific knowledge in the interests of the group is a feasible and promising possibility. Although we cannot say how

[11] B. F. Skinner, *Trans. N.Y. Acad. Sci.* 17, 547 (1955).

devious the course of its evolution may be, a cultural pattern of control and countercontrol will presumably emerge which will be most widely supported because it is most widely reinforcing.

If we cannot foresee all the details of this (as we obviously cannot), it is important to remember that this is true of the critics of science as well. The dire consequences of new techniques of control, the hidden menace in original cultural designs—these need some proof. It is only another example of my present point that the need for proof is so often overlooked. Man has got himself into some pretty fixes, and it is easy to believe that he will do so again. But there is a more optimistic possibility. The slow growth of the methods of science, now for the first time being applied to human affairs, *may* mean a new and exciting phase of human life to which historical analogies will not apply and in which earlier political slogans will not be appropriate. If we are to use the knowledge that a science of behavior is now making available with any hope of success, we must look at human nature as it is brought into focus through the methods of science rather than as it has been presented to us in a series of historical accidents.

If the advent of a powerful science of behavior causes trouble, it will not be because science itself is inimical to human welfare but because older conceptions have not yielded easily or gracefully. We expect resistance to new techniques of control from those who have heavy investments in the old, but we have no reason to help them preserve a series of principles that are not ends in themselves but rather outmoded means to an end. What is needed is a new conception of human behavior which is compatible with the implications of a scientific analysis. All men control and are controlled. The question of government in the broadest possible sense is not how freedom is to be preserved but what kinds of control are to be used and to what ends. Control must be analyzed and considered in its proper proportions. No one, I am sure, wishes to develop new master-slave relationships or bend the will of the people to despotic rulers in new ways. These are patterns of control appropriate to a world without science. They may well be the first to go when the experimental analysis of behavior comes into its own in the design of cultural practices.

II: Rogers

There are, I believe, a number of matters in connection with this important topic on which the authors of this article, and probably a large majority of psychologists, are in agreement. These matters then are not issues as far as we are concerned, and I should like to mention them briefly in order to put them to one side.

POINTS OF AGREEMENT

I am sure we agree that men—as individuals and as societies—have always endeavored to understand, predict, influence, and control human behavior—their own behavior and that of others.

I believe we agree that the behavioral sciences are

making and will continue to make increasingly rapid progress in the understanding of behavior, and that as a consequence the capacity to predict and to control behavior is developing with equal rapidity.

I believe we agree that to deny these advances, or to claim that man's behavior cannot be a field of science, is unrealistic. Even though this is not an issue for us, we should recognize that many intelligent men still hold strongly to the view that the actions of men are free in some sense such that scientific knowledge of man's behavior is impossible. Thus Reinhold Niebuhr, the noted theologian, heaps scorn on the concept of psychology as a science of man's behavior and even says, "In any event, no scientific investigation of past behavior can become the basis of predictions of future behavior."[12] So, while this is not an issue for psychologists, we should at least notice in passing that it is an issue for many people.

I believe we are in agreement that the tremendous potential power of a science which permits the prediction and control of behavior may be misused, and that the possibility of such misuse constitutes a serious threat.

Consequently Skinner and I are in agreement that the whole question of the scientific control of human behavior is a matter with which psychologists and the general public should concern themselves. As Robert Oppenheimer told the American Psychological Association in 1955[13] the problems that psychologists will

[12] R. Niebuhr, *The Self and the Dramas of History* (New York: Scribner, 1955), p. 47.

[13] R. Oppenheimer, *Am. Psychol.* *11*, 127 (1956).

pose for society by their growing ability to control behavior will be much more grave than the problems posed by the ability of physicists to control the reactions of matter. I am not sure whether psychologists generally recognize this. My impression is that by and large they hold a laissez-faire attitude. Obviously Skinner and I do not hold this laissez-faire view, or we would not have written this article.

POINTS AT ISSUE

With these several points of basic and important agreement, are there then any issues that remain on which there are differences? I believe there are. They can be stated very briefly: Who will be controlled? Who will exercise control? What type of control will be exercised? Most important of all, toward what end or what purpose, or in the pursuit of what value will control be exercised?

It is on questions of this sort that there exist ambiguities, misunderstandings, and probably deep differences. These differences exist among psychologists, among members of the general public in this country, and among various world cultures. Without any hope of achieving a final resolution of these questions, we can, I believe, put these issues in clearer form.

SOME MEANINGS

To avoid ambiguity and faulty communication, I would like to clarify the meanings of some of the terms we are using.

Behavioral science is a term that might be defined from several angles but in the context of this discussion it refers primarily to knowledge that the existence of certain describable conditions in the human being and/or in his environment is followed by certain describable consequences in his actions.

Prediction means the prior identification of behaviors which then occur. Because it is important in some things I wish to say later, I would point out that one may predict a highly specific behavior, such as an eye blink, or one may predict a class of behaviors. One might correctly predict "avoidant behavior," for example, without being able to specify whether the individual will run away or simply close his eyes.

The word *control* is a very slippery one, which can be used with any one of several meanings. I would like to specify three that seem most important for our present purposes. *Control* may mean: (1) The setting of conditions by *B* for *A*, *A* having no voice in the matter, such that certain predictable behaviors then occur in *A*. I refer to this as external control. (2) The setting of conditions by *B* for *A, A* giving some degree of consent to these conditions, such that certain predictable behaviors then occur in *A*. I refer to this as the influence of *B* on *A*. (3) The setting of conditions by *A* such that certain predictable behaviors then occur in himself. I refer to this as internal control. It will be noted that Skinner lumps together the first two meanings, external control and influence, under the concept of control. I find this confusing.

USUAL CONCEPT OF CONTROL OF HUMAN BEHAVIOR

With the underbrush thus cleared away (I hope), let us review very briefly the various elements that are involved in the usual concept of the control of human behavior as mediated by the behavioral sciences. I am drawing here on the previous writings of Skinner, on his present statements, on the writings of others who have considered in either friendly or antagonistic fashion the meanings that would be involved in such control. I have not excluded the science-fiction writers, as reported recently by Vandenburg,[14] since they often show an awareness of the issues involved, even though the methods described are as yet fictional. These then are the elements that seem common to these different concepts of the application of science to human behavior.

1) There must first be some sort of decision about goals. Usually desirable goals are assumed, but sometimes, as in George Orwell's book *1984*, the goal that is selected is an aggrandizement of individual power with which most of us would disagree. In a recent paper Skinner suggests that one possible set of goals to be assigned to the behavioral technology is this: "Let men be happy, informed, skillful, well-behaved and productive."[15] In the first draft of his part of this article, which he was kind enough to show me, he did not mention such definite goals as these, but de-

[14] S. G. Vandenburg, *ibid. 11*, 339 (1956).

[15] B. F. Skinner, *Am. Scholar 25*, 47 (1955–1956).

sired "improved" educational practices, "wiser" use of knowledge in government, and the like. In the final version of his article he avoids even these value-laden terms, and his implicit goal is the very general one that scientific control of behavior is desirable, because it would perhaps bring "a far better world for everyone."

Thus the first step in thinking about the control of human behavior is the choice of goals, whether specific or general. It is necessary to come to terms in some way with the issue, "For what purpose?"

2) A second element is that, whether the end selected is highly specific or is a very general one such as wanting "a better world," we proceed by the methods of science to discover the means to these ends. We continue through further experimentation and investigation to discover more effective means. The method of science is self-correcting in thus arriving at increasingly effective ways of achieving the purpose we have in mind.

3) The third aspect of such control is that, as the conditions or methods are discovered by which to reach the goal, some person or some group establishes these conditions and uses these methods, having in one way or another obtained the power to do so.

4) The fourth element is the exposure of individuals to the prescribed conditions, and this leads, with a high degree of probability, to behavior which is in line with the goals desired. Individuals are now happy, if that has been the goal, or well-behaved, or submissive, or whatever it has been decided to make them.

5) The fifth element is that if the process I have

described is put in motion then there is a continuing social organization which will continue to produce the types of behavior that have been valued.

SOME FLAWS

Are there any flaws in this way of viewing the control of human behavior? I believe there are. In fact the only element in this description with which I find myself in agreement is the second. It seems to me quite incontrovertibly true that the scientific method is an excellent way to discover the means by which to achieve our goals. Beyond that, I feel many sharp differences, which I will try to spell out.

I believe that in Skinner's presentation here, and in his previous writings, there is a serious underestimation of the problem of power. To hope that the power which is being made available by the behavioral sciences will be exercised by the scientists, or by a benevolent group, seems to me a hope little supported by either recent or distant history. It seems far more likely that behavioral scientists, holding their present attitudes, will be in the position of the German rocket scientists specializing in guided missiles. First they worked devotedly for Hitler to destroy the U.S.S.R. and the United States. Now, depending on who captured them, they work devotedly for the U.S.S.R. in the interest of destroying the United States, or devotedly for the United States in the interest of destroying the U.S.S.R. Concerned solely with advancing their science, it seems most probable that they will serve the purposes of whatever individual or group has the power.

But the major flaw I see in this review of what is involved in the scientific control of human behavior is the denial, misunderstanding, or gross underestimation of the place of ends, goals, or values in their relationship to science. This error (as it seems to me) has so many implications that I would like to devote some space to it.

ENDS AND VALUES IN RELATION TO SCIENCE

In sharp contradiction to some views that have been advanced, I would like to propose a two-pronged thesis: (1) In any scientific endeavor—whether "pure" or applied science—there is a prior subjective choice of the purpose or value which that scientific work is perceived as serving. (2) This subjective value choice which brings the scientific endeavor into being must always lie outside of that endeavor and can never become a part of the science involved in that endeavor.

Let me illustrate the first point from Skinner himself. It is clear that in his earlier writing[16] it is recognized that a prior value choice is necessary, and it is specified as the goal that men are to become happy, well-behaved, productive, and so on. I am pleased that Skinner has retreated from the goals he then chose, because to me they seem to be stultifying values. I can only feel that he was choosing these goals for others,

[16] *Ibid.*

not for himself. I would hate to see Skinner become "well-behaved," as that term would be defined for him by behavioral scientists. His recent article in the *American Psychologist*[17] shows that he certainly does not want to be "productive" as that value is defined by most psychologists. And the most awful fate I can imagine for him would be to have him constantly "happy." It is the fact that he is very unhappy about many things which makes me prize him.

In the first draft of his part of this article, he also included such prior value choices, saying for example, "We must decide how we are to use the knowledge which a science of human behavior is now making available." Now he has dropped all mention of such choices, and if I understand him correctly, he believes that science can proceed without them. He has suggested this view in another recent paper, stating that "We must continue to experiment in cultural design . . . testing the consequences as we go. Eventually the practices which make for the greatest biological and psychological strength of the group will presumably survive."[18]

I would point out, however, that to choose to experiment is a value choice. Even to move in the direction of perfectly random experimentation is a value choice. To test the consequences of an experiment is possible only if we have first made a subjective choice of a criterion value. And implicit in his statement is a valuing of biological and psychological strength. So even when trying to avoid such choice, it seems ines-

[17] B. F. Skinner, *Am. Psychol. 11,* 221 (1956).
[18] Skinner, *Trans. N.Y. Acad. Sci.,* p. 549.

capable that a prior subjective value choice is necessary for any scientific endeavor, or for any application of scientific knowledge.

I wish to make it clear that I am not saying that values cannot be included as a subject of science. It is not true that science deals only with certain classes of "facts" and that these classes do not include values. It is a bit more complex than that, as a simple illustration or two may make clear.

If I value knowledge of the "three Rs" as a goal of education, the methods of science can give me increasingly accurate information on how this goal may be achieved. If I value problem-solving ability as a goal of education, the scientific method can give me the same kind of help.

Now, if I wish to determine whether problem-solving ability is "better" than knowledge of the three Rs, then scientific method can also study those two values but *only*—and this is very important—in terms of some other value which I have subjectively chosen. I may value college success. Then I can determine whether problem-solving ability or knowledge of the three Rs is most closely associated with that value. I may value personal integration or vocational success or responsible citizenship. I can determine whether problem-solving ability or knowledge of the three Rs is "better" for achieving any one of these values. But the value or purpose that gives meaning to a particular scientific endeavor must always lie outside of that endeavor.

Although our concern in this symposium is largely with applied science, what I have been saying seems equally true of so-called pure science. In pure science the usual prior subjective value choice is the discovery of truth. But this is a subjective choice, and science can never say whether it is the best choice, save in the light of some other value. Geneticists in the U.S.S.R., for example, had to make a subjective choice of whether it was better to pursue truth or to discover facts which upheld a governmental dogma. Which choice is "better"? We could make a scientific investigation of those alternatives but only in the light of some other subjectively chosen value. If, for example, we value the survival of a culture, then we could begin to investigate with the methods of science the question of whether pursuit of truth or support of governmental dogma is most closely associated with cultural survival.

My point then is that any endeavor in science, pure or applied, is carried on in the pursuit of a purpose or value that is subjectively chosen by persons. It is important that this choice be made explicit, since the particular value which is being sought can never be tested or evaluated, confirmed or denied, by the scientific endeavor to which it gives birth. The initial purpose or value always and necessarily lies outside the scope of the scientific effort which it sets in motion.

Among other things this means that if we choose some particular goal or series of goals for human beings and then set out on a large scale to control human behavior to the end of achieving those goals, we are locked in the rigidity of our initial choice, because such a scientific endeavor can never transcend itself to select new goals. Only subjective human persons can do that. Thus if we chose as our goal the state of happiness for human beings (a goal deservedly ridiculed by Aldous Huxley in *Brave New World*), and if we involved all of society in a successful scientific program by which people became happy, we would be locked in a colossal rigidity in which no one would be free to question this goal, because our scientific operations could not transcend themselves to question their guiding purposes. And without laboring this point, I would remark that colossal rigidity, whether in dinosaurs or dictatorships, has a very poor record of evolutionary survival.

If, however, a part of our scheme is to set free some "planners" who do not have to be happy, who are not controlled, and who are therefore free to choose other values, this has several meanings. It means that the purpose we have chosen as our goal is not a sufficient and a satisfying one for human beings but must be supplemented. It also means that if it is necessary to set up an elite group which is free, then this shows all too clearly that the great majority are only the slaves—no matter by what high-sounding name we call them—of those who select the goals.

Perhaps, however, the thought is that a continuing scientific endeavor will evolve its own goals; that the initial findings will alter the directions, and subsequent findings will alter them still further, and that science somehow develops its own purpose. Although he does not clearly say so, this appears to be the pattern Skinner has in mind. It is surely a reasonable description, but it overlooks one element in this continuing development, which is that subjective personal choice enters in at every point at which the direction changes. The findings of a science, the results of an experiment, do not and never can tell us what next scientific purpose to pursue. Even in the purest of science, the scientist must decide what the findings mean and must subjectively choose what next step will be most profitable in the pursuit of his purpose. And if we are speaking of the application of scientific knowledge, then it is distressingly clear that the increasing scientific knowledge of the structure of the atom carries with it no necessary choice as to the purpose to which this knowledge will be put. This is a subjective personal choice which must be made by many individuals.

Thus I return to the proposition with which I began this section of my remarks—and which I now repeat in different words. Science has its meaning as the objective pursuit of a purpose which has been subjectively chosen by a person or persons. This purpose or value can never be investigated by the particular scientific experiment or investigation to which it has given birth and meaning. Consequently, any discussion of the control of human beings by the behavioral sciences must first and most deeply concern itself with the subjectively chosen purposes which such an application of science is intended to implement.

IS THE SITUATION HOPELESS?

The thoughtful reader may recognize that, although my remarks up to this point have introduced some modifications in the conception of the processes by which human behavior will be controlled, these remarks may have made such control seem, if anything, even more inevitable. We might sum it up this way: Behavioral science is clearly moving forward; the increasing power for control which it gives will be held by someone or some group; such an individual or group will surely choose the values or goals to be achieved; and most of us will then be increasingly controlled by means so subtle that we will not even be aware of them as controls. Thus, whether a council of wise psychologists (if this is not a contradiction in terms), or a Stalin, or a Big Brother has the power, and whether the goal is happiness, or productivity, or resolution of the Oedipus complex, or submission, or love of Big Brother, we will inevitably find ourselves moving toward the chosen goal and probably thinking that we ourselves desire it. Thus, if this line of reasoning is correct, it appears that some form of *Walden Two* or of *1984* (and at a deep philosophic level they seem indistinguishable) is coming. The fact that it would surely arrive piecemeal, rather than all at once, does not greatly change the fundamental issues. In any event, as Skinner has indicated in his writings, we would then look back upon the concepts of human freedom, the capacity for choice, the responsibility for choice, and the worth of the human individual as historical curiosities which once existed by cultural accident as values in a prescientific civilization.

I believe that any person observant of trends must regard something like the foregoing sequence as a real possibility. It is not simply a fantasy. Something of that sort may even be the most likely future. But is it an inevitable future? I want to devote the remainder of my remarks to an alternative possibility.

ALTERNATIVE SET OF VALUES

Suppose we start with a set of ends, values, purposes, quite different from the type of goals we have been considering. Suppose we do this quite openly, setting them forth as a possible value choice to be accepted or rejected. Suppose we select a set of values that focuses on fluid elements of process rather than static attributes. We might then value: man as a process of becoming, as a process of achieving worth and dignity through the development of his potentialities; the individual human being as a self-actualizing process, moving on to more challenging and enriching experiences; the process by which the individual creatively adapts to an ever-new and changing world; the process by which knowledge transcends itself, as, for example, the theory of relativity transcended Newtonian physics, itself to be transcended in some future day by a new perception.

If we select values such as these, we turn to our science and technology of behavior with a very different set of questions. We will want to know such things as these: Can science aid in the discovery of new modes of richly rewarding living? more meaningful and satisfying modes of interpersonal relationships? Can science inform us on how the human race can become a more intelligent participant in its own evolution—its physical, psychological, and social evolution? Can science inform us on ways of releasing the creative capacity of individuals, which seem so necessary if we are to survive in this fantastically expanding atomic age? Oppenheimer has pointed out[19] that knowledge, which used to double in millennia or centuries, now doubles in a generation or a decade. It appears that we must discover the utmost in release of creativity if we are to be able to adapt effectively. In short, can science discover the methods by which man can most readily become a continually developing and self-transcending process, in his behavior, his thinking, his knowledge? Can science predict and release an essentially "unpredictable" freedom?

It is one of the virtues of science as a method that it is as able to advance and implement goals and purposes of this sort as it is to serve static values, such as states of being well-informed, happy, obedient. Indeed we have some evidence of this.

SMALL EXAMPLE

I will perhaps be forgiven if I document some of the possibilities along this line by turning to psychotherapy, the field I know best.

Psychotherapy, as Meerloo[20] and others have pointed out, can be one of the most subtle tools for the control of *A* by *B*. The therapist can subtly mold individuals in imitation of himself. He can cause an individual to become a submissive and conforming being. When certain therapeutic principles are used in extreme

[19] R. Oppenheimer, *Roosevelt University Occasional Papers* 2 (1956).

[20] J. A. M. Meerloo, *J. Nervous Mental Disease* 122, 353 (1955).

fashion, we call it brainwashing, an instance of the disintegration of the personality and a reformulation of the person along lines desired by the controlling individual. So the principles of therapy can be used as an effective means of external control of human personality and behavior. Can psychotherapy be anything else?

Here I find the developments going on in client-centered psychotherapy[21] an exciting hint of what a behavioral science can do in achieving the kinds of values I have stated. Quite aside from being a somewhat new orientation in psychotherapy, this development has important implications regarding the relation of a behavioral science to the control of human behavior. Let me describe our experience as it relates to the issues of this discussion.

In client-centered therapy we are deeply engaged in the prediction and influencing of behavior, or even the control of behavior. As therapists, we institute certain attitudinal conditions, and the client has relatively little voice in the establishment of these conditions. We predict that if these conditions are instituted, certain behavioral consequences will ensue in the client. Up to this point this is largely external control, no different from what Skinner has described, and no different from what I have discussed in the preceding sections of this article. But here any similarity ceases.

The conditions we have chosen to establish predict such behavioral consequences as these: that the client

[21] C. R. Rogers, *Client-Centered Therapy* (Boston: Houghton Mifflin, 1951).

will become self-directing, less rigid, more open to the evidence of his senses, better organized and integrated, more similar to the ideal which he has chosen for himself. In other words, we have established by external control conditions which I predict will be followed by internal control by the individual, in pursuit of externally chosen goals. We have set the conditions which predict various classes of behaviors—self-directing behaviors, sensitivity to realities within and without, flexible adaptiveness—which are by their very nature unpredictable in their specifics. Our recent research[22] indicates that our predictions are to a significant degree corroborated, and our commitment to the scientific method causes us to believe that more effective means of achieving these goals may be realized.

Research exists in other fields—industry, education, group dynamics—which seems to support our own findings. I believe it may be conservatively stated that scientific progress has been made in identifying those conditions in an interpersonal relationship which, if they exist in *B*, are followed in *A* by greater maturity in behavior, less dependence on others, an increase in expressiveness as a person, an increase in variability, flexibility, and effectiveness of adaptation, an increase in self-responsibility and self-direction. And, quite in contrast to the concern expressed by some, we do not find that the creatively adaptive behavior which results from such self-directed variability of expression is a

[22] C. R. Rogers and R. Dymond, eds., *Psychotherapy and Personality Change* (Chicago: University of Chicago Press, 1954).

"happy accident" which occurs in "chaos." Rather, the individual who is open to his experience, and self-directing, is harmonious not chaotic, ingenious rather than random, as he orders his responses imaginatively toward the achievement of his own purposes. His creative actions are no more a "happy accident" than was Einstein's development of the theory of relativity.

Thus we find ourselves in fundamental agreement with John Dewey's statement: "Science has made its way by releasing, not by suppressing, the elements of variation, of invention and innovation, of novel creation in individuals."[23] Progress in personal life and in group living is, we believe, made in the same way.

POSSIBLE CONCEPT OF THE CONTROL OF HUMAN BEHAVIOR

It is quite clear that the point of view I am expressing is in sharp contrast to the usual conception of the relationship of the behavioral sciences to the control of human behavior. In order to make this contrast even more blunt, I will state this possibility in paragraphs parallel to those used before.

1) It is possible for us to choose to value man as a self-actualizing process of becoming; to value creativity, and the process by which knowledge becomes self-transcending.

2) We can proceed, by the methods of science, to discover the conditions which necessarily precede these processes and, through continuing experimenta-

[23] J. Ratner, ed., *Intelligence in the Modern World: John Dewey's Philosophy* (New York: Modern Library, 1939), p. 359.

tion, to discover better means of achieving these purposes.

3) It is possible for individuals or groups to set these conditions, with a minimum of power or control. According to present knowledge, the only authority necessary is the authority to establish certain qualities of interpersonal relationship.

4) Exposed to these conditions, present knowledge suggests that individuals become more self-responsible, make progress in self-actualization, become more flexible, and become more creatively adaptive.

5) Thus such an initial choice would inaugurate the beginnings of a social system or subsystem in which values, knowledge, adaptive skills, and even the concept of science would be continually changing and self-transcending. The emphasis would be upon man as a process of becoming.

I believe it is clear that such a view as I have been describing does not lead to any definable utopia. It would be impossible to predict its final outcome. It involves a step-by-step development, based on a continuing subjective choice of purposes, which are implemented by the behavioral sciences. It is in the direction of the *open society,* as that term has been defined by Popper,[24] where individuals carry responsibility for personal decisions. It is at the opposite pole from his concept of the closed society, of which *Walden Two* would be an example.

I trust it is also evident that the whole emphasis is on process, not on end states of being. I am suggesting

[24] K. R. Popper, *The Open Society and Its Enemies* (London: Routledge and Kegan Paul, 1945).

that it is by choosing to value certain qualitative elements of the process of becoming that we can find a pathway toward the open society.

THE CHOICE

It is my hope that we have helped to clarify the range of choice which will lie before us and our children in regard to the behavioral sciences. We can choose to use our growing knowledge to enslave people in ways never dreamed of before, depersonalizing them, controlling them by means so carefully selected that they will perhaps never be aware of their loss of personhood. We can choose to utilize our scientific knowledge to make men happy, well-behaved, and productive, as Skinner earlier suggested. Or we can insure that each person learns all the syllabus which we select and set before him, as Skinner now suggests. Or at the other end of the spectrum of choice we can choose to use the behavioral sciences in ways which will free, not control; which will bring about constructive variability, not conformity; which will develop creativity, not contentment; which will facilitate each person in his self-directed process of becoming; which will aid individuals, groups, and even the concept of science to become self-transcending in freshly adaptive ways of meeting life and its problems. The choice is up to us, and, the human race being what it is, we are likely to stumble about, making at times some nearly disastrous value choices and at other times highly constructive ones.

I am aware that to some, this setting forth of a choice is unrealistic, because a choice of values is regarded as not possible. Skinner has stated:

> Man's vaunted creative powers . . . his capacity to choose and our right to hold him responsible for his choice—none of these is conspicuous in this new self-portrait (provided by science). Man, we once believed, was free to express himself in art, music, and literature, to inquire into nature, to seek salvation in his own way. He could initiate action and make spontaneous and capricious changes of course. . . . But science insists that action is initiated by forces impinging upon the individual, and that caprice is only another name for behavior for which we have not yet found a cause.[25]

I can understand this point of view, but I believe that it avoids looking at the great paradox of behavioral science. Behavior, when it is examined scientifically, is surely best understood as determined by prior causation. This is one great fact of science. But responsible personal choice, which is the most essential element in being a person, which is the core experience in psychotherapy, which exists prior to any scientific endeavor, is an equally prominent fact in our lives. To deny the experience of responsible choice is, to me, as restricted a view as to deny the possibility of a behavioral science. That these two important elements of our experience appear to be in contradiction has perhaps the same significance as the contradiction between the wave theory and the corpuscular theory of light, both of which can be shown to be true, even

[25] Skinner, *Am. Scholar 25*, 52–53.

though incompatible. We cannot profitably deny our subjective life, any more than we can deny the objective description of that life.

In conclusion then, it is my contention that science cannot come into being without a personal choice of the values we wish to achieve. And these values we choose to implement will forever lie outside of the science which implements them; the goals we select, the purposes we wish to follow, must always be outside of the science which achieves them. To me this has the encouraging meaning that the human person, with his capacity of subjective choice, can and will always exist, separate from and prior to any of his scientific undertakings. Unless as individuals and groups we choose to relinquish our capacity of subjective choice, we will always remain persons, not simply pawns of a self-created science.

III: Skinner

I cannot quite agree that the practice of science *requires* a prior decision about goals or a prior choice of values. The metallurgist can study the properties of steel and the engineer can design a bridge without raising the question of whether a bridge is to be built. But such questions are certainly frequently raised and tentatively answered. Rogers wants to call the answers "subjective choices of values." To me, such an expression suggests that we have had to abandon more rigorous scientific practices in order to talk about our own behavior. In the experimental analysis of other organisms I would use other terms, and I shall try to do so here. Any list of values is a list of reinforcers—conditioned or otherwise. We are so constituted that under certain circumstances food, water, sexual contact, and so on will make any behavior which produces them more likely to occur again. Other things may acquire this power. We do not need to say that an organism chooses to eat rather than to starve. If you answer that it is a very different thing when a man chooses to starve, I am only too happy to agree. If it were not so, we should have cleared up the question of choice long ago. An organism can be reinforced by —can be made to "choose"—almost any given state of affairs.

Rogers is concerned with choices that involve multiple and usually conflicting consequences. I have dealt with some of these elsewhere[26] in an analysis of self-control. Shall I eat these delicious strawberries today if I will then suffer an annoying rash tomorrow? The decision I am to make used to be assigned to the province of ethics. But we are now studying similar combinations of positive and negative consequences, as well as collateral conditions which affect the result in the laboratory. Even a pigeon can be taught some measure of self-control! And this work helps us to understand the operation of certain formulas—among them value judgments—which folk wisdom, religion, and psychotherapy have advanced in the interests of self-discipline. The observable effect of any statement of value is to alter the relative effectiveness of reinforcers. We may no longer enjoy the strawberries for

[26] B. F. Skinner, *Science and Human Behavior* (New York: Macmillan, 1953).

thinking about the rash. If rashes are made sufficiently shameful, illegal, sinful, maladjusted, or unwise, we may glow with satisfaction as we push the strawberries aside in a grandiose avoidance response which would bring a smile to the lips of Murray Sidman.

People behave in ways which, as we say, conform to ethical, governmental, or religious patterns because they are reinforced for doing so. The resulting behavior may have far-reaching consequences for the survival of the pattern to which it conforms. And whether we like it or not, survival is the ultimate criterion. This is where, it seems to me, science can help —not in choosing a goal, but in enabling us to predict the survival value of cultural practices. Man has too long tried to get the kind of world he wants by glorifying some brand of immediate reinforcement. As science points up more and more of the remoter consequences, he may begin to work to strengthen behavior, not in a slavish devotion to a chosen value, but with respect to the ultimate survival of mankind. Do not ask me why I want mankind to survive. I can tell you why only in the sense in which the physiologist can tell you why I want to breathe. Once the relation between a given step and the survival of my group has been pointed out, I will take that step. And it is the business of science to point out just such relations.

The values I have occasionally recommended (and Rogers has not led me to recant) are transitional. Other things being equal, I am betting on the group whose practices make for healthy, happy, secure, productive, and creative people. And I insist that the values recommended by Rogers are transitional, too, for I can ask him the same kind of question. Man as a process of becoming—*what?* Self-actualization—for what? Inner control is no more a goal than external.

What Rogers seems to me to be proposing, both here and elsewhere,[27] is this: Let us use our increasing power of control to create individuals who will not need and perhaps will no longer respond to control. Let us solve the problem of our power by renouncing it. At first blush this seems as implausible as a benevolent despot. Yet power has occasionally been forsworn. A nation has burned its Reichstag, rich men have given away their wealth, beautiful women have become ugly hermits in the desert, and psychotherapists have become non-directive. When this happens, I look to other possible reinforcements for a plausible explanation. People relinquish democratic power when a tyrant promises them the earth. Rich men give away wealth to escape the accusing finger of their fellowmen. A woman destroys her beauty in the hope of salvation. And a psychotherapist relinquishes control because he can thus help his client more effectively.

The solution that Rogers is suggesting is thus understandable. But is he correctly interpreting the result? What evidence is there that a client ever becomes truly *self*-directing? What evidence is there that he ever makes a truly *inner* choice of ideal or goal? Even though the therapist does not do the choosing, even though he encourages "self-actualization"—he is not out of control as long as he holds himself ready to step in when occasion demands—when, for example, the

[27] Rogers, *Teachers College Record.*

client chooses the goal of becoming a more accomplished liar or murdering his boss. But supposing the therapist does withdraw completely or is no longer necessary—what about all the other forces acting upon the client? Is the self-chosen goal independent of his early ethical and religious training? of the folk wisdom of his group? of the opinions and attitudes of others who are important to him? Surely not. The therapeutic situation is only a small part of the world of the client. From the therapist's point of view it may appear to be possible to relinquish control. But the control passes, not to a "self," but to forces in other parts of the client's world. The solution of the therapist's problem of power cannot be *our* solution, for we must consider *all* the forces acting upon the individual.

The child who must be prodded and nagged is something less than a fully developed human being. We want to see him hurrying to his appointment, not because each step is taken in response to verbal reminders from his mother, but because certain temporal contingencies, in which dawdling has been punished and hurrying reinforced, have worked a change in his behavior. Call this a state of better organization, a greater sensitivity to reality, or what you will. The plain fact is that the child passes from a temporary verbal control exercised by his parents to control by certain inexorable features of the environment. I should suppose that something of the same sort happens in successful psychotherapy. Rogers seems to me to be saying this: Let us put an end, as quickly as possible, to any pattern of master and slave, to any direct obedience to command, to the submissive following of suggestions. Let the individual be free to adjust himself to more rewarding features of the world about him. In the end, let his teachers and counselors "wither away," like the Marxist state. I not only agree with this as a useful ideal, I have constructed a fanciful world to demonstrate its advantages. It saddens me to hear Rogers say that "at a deep philosophic level" *Walden Two* and George Orwell's *1984* "seem indistinguishable." They could scarcely be more unlike—at any level. The book *1984* is a picture of immediate aversive control for vicious selfish purposes. The founder of *Walden Two,* on the other hand, has built a community in which neither he nor any other person exerts any *current* control. His achievement lay in his original *plan,* and when he boasts of this ("It is enough to satisfy the thirstiest tyrant"), we do not fear him but only pity him for his weakness.

Another critic of *Walden Two,* Andrew Hacker,[28] has discussed this point in considering the bearing of mass conditioning upon the liberal notion of autonomous man. In drawing certain parallels between the Grand Inquisition passage in Dostoevsky's *Brothers Karamazov,* Huxley's *Brave New World,* and *Walden Two,* he attempts to set up a distinction to be drawn in any society between conditioners and conditioned. He assumes that "the conditioner can be said to be autonomous in the traditional liberal sense." But then he notes: "Of course the conditioner has been conditioned. But he has not been conditioned by the conscious manipulation of another *person.*" But how does this affect the resulting behavior? Can we not soon forget

[28] A. Hacker, *J. Politics 17,* 590 (1955).

the origins of the "artificial" diamond which is identical with the real thing? Whether it is an "accidental" cultural pattern, such as is said to have produced the founder of *Walden Two,* or the engineered environment which is about to produce his successors, we are dealing with sets of conditions generating human behavior which will ultimately be measured by their contribution to the strength of the group. We look to the future, not the past, for the test of "goodness" or acceptability.

If we are worthy of our democratic heritage we shall, of course, be ready to resist any tyrannical use of science for immediate or selfish purposes. But if we value the achievements and goals of democracy we must not refuse to apply science to the design and construction of cultural patterns, even though we may then find ourselves in some sense in the position of controllers. Fear of control, generalized beyond any warrant, has led to a misinterpretation of valid practices and the blind rejection of intelligent planning for a better way of life. In terms which I trust Rogers will approve, in conquering this fear we shall become more mature and better organized and shall, thus, more fully actualize ourselves as human beings.

PART I

REACTIONS TO VARIOUS PSYCHOLOGICAL CONCEPTS

Motivation

Perception

Learning

The Freudian Model
and the Unconscious

Overview | In this section, Dr. Rogers and I discuss some basic psychological concepts or theories, so the reader can place Dr. Rogers' approach in perspective. Dr. Rogers reacts to more traditional psychological concepts of motivation, perception, and learning. Finally, we discuss the Freudian model of personality and the unconscious.

EVANS: Dr. Rogers, to begin our discussion, I'd like to relate some of your views to three of the important dimensions that are almost always dealt with in psychology—motivation, perception, and learning. Beginning with motivation, in psychology we have tended to define this as all conditions which arouse, direct, and sustain the organism. This generally is interpreted as a homeostatic model, taken from biology—that the organism seeks to reduce tensions and maintain a state of equilibrium. I gather that your theory is not developed out of this particular approach to motivation. Is that correct?

ROGERS: Yes, I do not agree with that point of view because I think the organism is definitely not trying to achieve *stasis*. I think that even organisms as low as the flatworm are always trying to look for more enriching stimuli, more complicated stimuli, and so that homeostatic approach is not very congenial with my point.

EVANS: In other words, in not accepting this homeostatic

model, you feel that man is almost striving for tensions rather than seeking to reduce his tensions?

ROGERS: Always. I think there is plenty of evidence now that this is true. In man, we call it curiosity. In lower animals, it's a tendency to seek more complicated stimuli rather than simple ones.

EVANS: The late Abraham Maslow talked about a hierarchy of needs, starting with the striving for satisfaction of physiological needs and safety needs and moving all the way up to a higher order such as the need for self-actualization. This also seems to reflect a homeostatic model. Would you say that even Maslow's motivational system, which has sometimes been compared to yours, is not agreeable to you?

ROGERS: Well, no, there is a tendency to satisfy needs, I would agree with that—but that isn't all there is. Homeostasis is not the ultimate direction of the individual. That's really what I'm saying.

EVANS: Let's look at needs as they have been studied in psychology. There have been attempts to look at very specific needs, attempts to develop an understanding of how they come about and develop. For example, McClelland (1953) deals with the need for achievement. This, of course, is borrowed from Henry Murray's (1938) original formulation that man seems to have this need as he develops socially—to achieve, to more or less be successful, to master his environment. The notion which McClelland and Atkinson pursued in their work was that the strength of this need might come from early childhood experience. For example, they argue that perhaps early independence training of a child will lead to high needs for achievement later in life. Do you think there is a value to psychology in taking a specific need and tracing back to early childhood patterns that contribute to its development?

ROGERS: No, I think it was of value to McClelland and I think there is truth, some truth, in all such approaches. However, rather than try to comment on such approaches to motivation, I'd rather say something about my own view of motivation. For instance, here in my garden, I was showing you some begonias that I raise. I might ask what "motivates" a begonia to grow from a little two-inch bulb to these really beautiful plants and flowers. It seems to me we could say it must be a need for achievement because some of those blooms, in their prime, are nine inches across. We say there's a sex drive because the male and female flowers grow on the same flower stalk. Well, of course, that's poppycock and I think it's pretty much poppycock in regard to human beings as well. The much more basic thing is that every organism has a tendency to maintain itself, to enhance itself if possible, eventually to reproduce itself. To me, that basic tendency toward growth, toward maintaining and enhancing the organism, is the central aspect of all motivation. Now, you can say, yes, and some of that seems to be describable as a need for achievement and so it certainly is channeled into a sexual drive, and so forth. I'd prefer to emphasize what to me is much more basic than any of those single concepts.

EVANS: Of course, the homeostatic model to which you have been taking some exception was basic to Freudian theory. Since so many writers have cited your work as an "alternative to Freud," it would be interesting to get your reactions to some of Freud's views. Let's start with his construct of the unconscious. Particularly in his early work, Freud (1953) seemed to see man as primarily irrational rather than rational in the sense that most of man's behavior is unconsciously determined. In fact, he introduces the concept of *overdeterminism,* which suggests that man does nothing by accident—that everything he does has unconscious determinants. How do you regard this construct of the unconscious?

ROGERS: I think that I see the same sort of phenomena that Freud saw, for which he developed this concept. I think that psychologists in general, and perhaps psychology students especially, tend to make things out of these concepts when they are really attempts by someone to understand an observable set of phenomena. I'd prefer to think of a range of phenomena: first, those in sharp focus in awareness right now—the height of consciousness; secondly, a range of material which could be called into consciousness, that you really know and can call into consciousness but you don't have in "figure" right now—it is in the "ground" or background; then, finally, some phenomena which are more and more dimly connected with awareness, to material that is really prevented from coming into even vague awareness because its coming into awareness would damage the person's concept of himself.

EVANS: So in a way, you're redefining Freud's views of the unconscious in a more rational sense.

ROGERS: Yes. You see, I feel that whether or not I

totally agree or disagree with Freud's concept of the unconscious is, in itself, not very helpful. I'd rather point out that the way I conceptualize the same kind of phenomena is along this spectrum I just mentioned: a continuum from material that is sharply in focus to the individual at the immediate moment to material that would be too threatening to even permit into the awareness at all.

EVANS: While we're discussing specific needs, you mentioned sexual motivation. Freud, of course, emphasized sexual motivation heavily, particularly in his early work. His classic model of psychosexual development has been very influential. As you know, this model postulates that in the first five years of life there is a progression of experiences that are related to the biological-sexual unfolding of the individual. He developed the notion of the "repetition compulsion," that the individual seemed to be affected over and over again by those early childhood sexual experiences, such as those with the opposite-sex parent. How do you feel about this notion?

ROGERS: Well, I think that there is a germ of truth in all of that. Freud was very much a creature of his time in placing great stress on the sexual aspect of development. Personally, I would be more concerned with the development of the whole concept of self in the individual as he grows. To be sure, the individual is influenced by attitudes and values and perceptions which he interjects from significant figures in his early life and all the way on up. However, I think that it's somewhat artificial to divide the development of the child into hard-and-fast stages. A gradual development of the picture that he carries of himself is more important to me than focusing on merely the sexual aspect of it.

EVANS: Do you feel that these early childhood experiences can continue to determine the individual's behavior over and over again? Do you think they are that powerful in their impact?

ROGERS: Yes, I think that early experience is a powerful force. Attitudes and values that are interjected from the parent do have a continuing influence and consequently would repeatedly influence behavior. You see, all along through here, I'm objecting to putting hard-and-fast labels on these processes. I don't like the pigeonholes that Freudian and other theories have promulgated. I think people handicap their thinking when they think in terms of so many labels. I'd rather they observe the phenomena themselves.

EVANS: Moving away from our brief discussion of motivation, I mentioned earlier another central area in psychology—perception. You are certainly aware of the rather interesting developments in the area of perception in the last few years. From an interest in the more precise studies of perception, which merely emphasized the study of sensory processes by relating the individual's response to a very specific stimulus, we have moved to examining the individual's overall experience in its more naïve, natural state. We have moved toward phenomenology, the sort of thing that William James called "stream of consciousness." Of course, the philosophers who discuss phenomenology would say that we are only superficially approaching what they are talking about. This phenomenological approach of the study of the total, naïve, immediate experience of the individual is more interesting to many psychologists today than very precise reactions to specific stimuli. Is this movement to phenomenology in line with your own interests?

ROGERS: Yes, very definitely. I think that I am really characteristic of the trend you mentioned. I recognize the narrow field of perception as a neurological event very worthy of study, but it is of relatively little interest to me. I am more interested in the Gestalt of what the person perceives in his environment and in himself. One thing that seems very true to me is that there is no such thing as a perception without a meaning. That is, the human organism immediately attaches a meaning to whatever is perceived. I may, out of the corner of my eye, see a plane in the distance. But if I turn my head that way, I discover it's a little gnat flying close by. In other words, in each case I attach a meaning to that perception immediately, even though it may be an erroneous meaning, as in the first case. For me, the perception is reality as far as the individual is concerned. I don't even know whether there is an objective reality. Probably there is, but none of us ever really knows that. All we know is what we perceive, and we try to test that in various ways. If it seems to be perceived in the same way from several different aspects, we regard it as real. The world of reality for the individual is his own field of perception, with the meanings he has attached to those various aspects. Probably any organism, certainly the human organism, is always trying to satisfy its needs as they are experienced in the phenomenological field—that is, the world about him as he perceives it, in the reality as he perceives it.

EVANS: You appear to be agreeing with Immanuel Kant who suggested that there is no reality except in terms of man's perception of it.

ROGERS: Yes, I am. I have tried stating that sometimes and find that it always leads to fruitless arguments, so I don't say so very often. But, as you suggest, it really fits in with my response to your earlier comment. None of us knows for sure what constitutes objective reality and we live our whole lives in the reality as perceived.

EVANS: We've briefly discussed motivation and perception, two central constructs in psychology. Another fundamental construct is learning. It's clear from looking at your work that you have not ignored learning and have been very interested in it. As in perception, there is a spectrum in learning theories. At one end, we have what might be called cognitive learning, which emphasizes the individual's experiences and cognitions and their development and organization. The other extreme attempts to stress the behavior of the organism rather than its experience and cognitions. On the one hand, we have psychologists such as the late E. C. Tolman (1932), interested in the organism's cognitive state in a stimulus-organism-response model; and on the other we have behaviorists such as the late Clark Hull (1943), interested merely in the stimulus-response segment; and B. F. Skinner (1971), in a sense, interested primarily in the response of the organism. Obviously, you would be more in agreement with the Tolmanian view, emphasizing cognition rather than the highly behavior-centered theories. You would be more interested in the individual's experience as we study learning and would not be content to focus primarily on behavior. Is that correct?

ROGERS: Yes, I certainly would be closer to that view. I've never been particularly interested in the atomistic theories of learning. I used to think when the molecular S-R theories, such as Hull's, were in vogue that learning theory was a very boring subject. However, I think that the kind of view that I have of learning is not entirely cognitive, either. I think it is holistic, that the individual learns as a whole, which includes the nature of the stimulus and the response as well as the individual's cognition and affect. As I mentioned earlier, this desire to enrich the stimuli with which one is faced is a very deep desire. Out of it grows our whole desire for play. I have known prominent scientists who are strongly motivated by that notion of play. They like to play with new ideas, new theories, new possibilities, new hunches. It's like a small child who is continuously on the go, on the move. That's one reason why the child is so hard to manage and get along with. It's because he's continually trying to learn about his environment in all sorts of ways, some of which don't quite fit in with adult notions. I think this desire for learning, this desire to grasp something that is meaningful to the self, to the person at the moment, is something that needs to be nurtured rather than molded. That's why I grow a little fearful of some of the possible results of the use of Skinner's theory, which you mentioned, and his notion of "operant conditioning," which focuses primarily on modifying the behavior of the organism. Skinner's contribution has been a major one in many ways, but it also has somewhat frightening aspects. I would like to see, instead, individuals encouraged to follow their own deep desire to learn, to enrich, to grow, to create. That's what I think is the most essential part of learning. Rather than being planned, as Skinner would have it, I believe that learning should be highly spontaneous and should occur as the person feels that which is to be learned is related to his own needs and his own desire to enhance himself.

EVANS: So, aren't you saying somewhat the same thing about learning that you said about perception? The precise study and analysis of this process is not the really important factor because the learning process is more complex than more precise analysis can reveal.

ROGERS: Well, you're giving one definition to precision. I think that we can make precise studies of complex phenomena, too. I would be interested in seeing more precise studies of the way in which the human being reaches out to grasp material which has meaning to him. But I think that to be precise in the atomistic fashion is a matter of less interest.

PART II

ROGERS' CONCEPTION OF THE SELF

Self-Actualization

Real Self *vs.* Ideal Self

Congruence *vs.* Incongruence

Overview | Perhaps one of the central constructs in Carl Rogers' approach to personality is the self. In this section, Dr. Rogers and I discuss the evolution of his conception of the self, and specifically discuss such constructs as self-actualization, the real self as related to the ideal self, and Rogers' conceptions of congruence-incongruence.

EVANS: In looking more specifically at some of the principal ideas with which you deal in your own writings and research over the years, it seems that you were among the earliest group of individuals in psychology to stress the self. You've already mentioned the concept of self in your answers to some of these other questions. Of course, self may be defined in many ways. What does the concept of self mean to you?

ROGERS: I think I might lead up to that by saying why I became interested in that particular construct. I certainly didn't start psychological work being interested in anything as vague as the self. To me, that seemed like old-fashioned introspectionism. I was really forced to examine self and forced to define it for myself, because my clients in therapy kept using that term in all kinds of significant ways. They'd say, "I think I've got a pretty solid self underneath this kind of phony exterior" or, "I'd be terribly afraid of getting to know my real self." They showed in all kinds of ways that, for them, self was a significant construct. I couldn't decide whether it was significant for them. I felt I should take a more direct look at it. To me, the self includes all of the individual's perceptions of his organism, of his experience, and of the way in which those perceptions are related to other perceptions and objects in his environment and to the whole exterior world.

EVANS: In the history of psychology, many individuals such as Carl Jung (Evans, 1964), as he discussed the individuation process, viewed the self in terms of a process of growth toward an actualization. Kurt Goldstein (1939) formulated this notion in his concept of self-actualization. Your view of the self also takes into account this notion of growth, does it not?

ROGERS: Yes. Ideally, the organism is always endeavoring to actualize itself. Of course, this is what I was referring to earlier when we discussed motivation. When the self is aware of what is going on in the organism, then it keeps changing, growing, and developing in the same way that the organism does. In most of us, the static aspects of the self are what really constitute maladjustment. Maladjustment would result if I persist in holding a set view of myself which doesn't correspond with what's actually going on in my organism. An extreme example relates to a boy I knew a long time ago. He had been raised in a very strictly religious home. He had no sex feelings or sex desires that were a part of his self-picture. I saw him because he was arrested for lifting the skirts of little girls. In other words, his organism was experiencing all kinds of sexual curiosity and desire, but as far as his self-picture was concerned, that was not a part of it at all. When he was arrested, he said that it couldn't have been him and that he couldn't have done it. In the strictly technical sense, his self-picture couldn't do it, and didn't do it. In that sense, he was right, as his organism was experiencing all these drives and acting on them. Now, to change that to a picture of adjustment, he would need to be aware of it and accept his sexual drive as well as the other aspects of himself. Then his picture of himself would match what was going on within his organism, and I would say that he would then be much closer to psychological adjustment. Self-actualization implies that the person is acceptantly aware of what's going on within and is consequently changing practically every moment and is moving on in complexity.

EVANS: Are you really suggesting that a balance among the "selves" that may exist in the person is somehow achieved?

ROGERS: Yes, but it should be mentioned that some students of mine stressed too much, perhaps, the notion of different selves, although I don't quarrel with that idea particularly. This idea hasn't had as much meaning for me as the notion of a more complex unified picture of self which keeps expanding to include new experiences, even though some experiences may be shut out as being too threatening. It seems that each of us endeavors to preserve the concept or picture that he has of himself and that a sharp change in that picture is quite threatening. Any change destroys some of the security that we feel we need. Using the example of the little boy that I just mentioned, it would be very threatening to his concept of the self to be faced with the fact that he had strong sexual desires, and they're not all social ones, either. That would literally bowl him over. What does he do? He shuts out of awareness any of his behavior, or feelings, or attitudes that would destroy a portion of his self concept. We all are quite capable of doing this. That really is what therapy is all about—to help drop the barrier so that a person can realize, "Yes, I do have these parts of myself and parts of my experience that I have hitherto thought were totally unacceptable."

EVANS: In this same respect, how would you relate your terms *ideal self* versus *real self* to our discussion?

ROGERS: Those terms grew up in an attempt to measure the self perception. I might say that one reason I was so reluctant to use the concept of the self was that if I got into something that vague, it could never be measured. We could never do research on the self. That's why William Stephenson's (1953) development of the Q-sort[1] came along at just the right moment, as far as I was concerned. Here was a way of getting an objective picture of this highly subjective phenomenon—the self. Then we realized that a person does not value every aspect of himself, so we asked the subjects in our research to sort the Q cards for a picture of the self they would like to be, which gave a picture of the ideal self as compared with the self as currently perceived. That proved to be quite a valuable way of bringing objectivity into the study of this

[1] In this procedure the subject is given a series of statements on which he or she is asked to evaluate himself or herself by placing them in several piles: pile A = most like himself or herself; pile B = next most like himself or herself, etc.

ephemeral phenomenon. When you get the valued self as against the currently perceived self, all kinds of interesting comparisons can be made.

EVANS: Based on your description of the self, there are obviously certain important resolutions that the human organism must undergo. To delve a bit more deeply into this, you have introduced an interesting polarity—congruence versus incongruence—to describe this process of integration of self and experience. What do you actually mean by congruency versus incongruency?

ROGERS: Incongruence results when the individual's experience is quite discrepant from the way he has organized himself. A common example is the person who is convinced that he's intellectually inferior. He may actually do creative and good things that show he has a fine intellect, but he can't believe those. The discrepancy between the picture he has of himself and what he is actually experiencing is called incongruence. What we are working toward in counseling or therapy is a greater congruence of self and experience, so that the individual is able to be aware of what he's experiencing, which means that he is not too defensively organized. He's able to be aware of even things which might change his concept of himself and can organize those into the Gestalt of the experience in regard to self. The term may also be used in relationship to congruence in the therapist, which is very important in the relationship. It is very important for the therapist to be himself in the therapeutic relationship. He, too, may be an incongruent person in other ways, but it's important that in the therapeutic relationship he should be what he is experiencing. Otherwise, he comes across to the client as a little bit phony or somewhat of a facade, and therapy is not nearly so likely to take place. So one description I've given of what it means to be congruent in a given moment is to be aware of what's going on in your experiencing at that moment, to be acceptant toward that experience, to be able to voice it if it's appropriate, and to express it in some behavioral way.

PSYCHOTHERAPY

PART III

Overview | When Carl Rogers systemized his "non-directive" or "client-centered" approach to psychotherapy, a dramatic reconsideration of earlier approaches to counseling and psychotherapy occurred. In this section, Dr. Rogers and I discuss this approach to therapy in general, and the specific techniques he employs. We also discuss psychoanalysis, group psychotherapy, and the so-called personal growth or encounter-group movement.

EVANS: You've introduced the notion of psychotherapy in your answer to my last question, Dr. Rogers, and this leads us to an obvious area of discussion. Your work has had such visible impact, it would be difficult to find anyone who has ever had any contact with any profession relating to interpersonal relationships who is not aware of it. In your book, *Counseling and Psychotherapy* (Rogers, 1942), you were talking about nondirective counseling, and as time passed, you began using terms like *client-centered* psychotherapy. Can you trace in more detail the evolution of this important contribution?

ROGERS: I guessed you might be raising some questions along that line, and I was thinking about it in terms of the books that I've written. It really goes back further than you mentioned, because my book, *Clinical Treatment of the Problem Child,* which was really written in 1936 and 1937 and published in 1939, shows where I stood at that point. I was working with children then and my whole aim was to manipulate the conditions under which the child lived, so as to improve his adjustment. We made a diagnosis of the child's situation. We developed a treatment plan. We brought in all the different agencies, the school, the courts, whatever was needed to make sure that the plan was carried through. So that shows my approach at that time, at least to the child, was on the whole, a planful but basically manipulative approach. But you'll find traces in that book of a beginning notion of something a little more than that, which attempted to get in touch with the individual client with whom one is dealing. Then by 1942 when *Counseling and Psychotherapy* came out, quite a little of that was still directed negatively: "Don't diagnose, don't advise, don't interpret." The central theme was the notion that the potential for better health resided in the client, and it certainly was quite a technique-oriented book. The counselor's responses were to be of the sort which would enable the client's potential to develop. Then *Client-Centered Therapy* was written in 1949 and 1950 and published in 1951. There the hypothesis was becoming a little more sophisticated—that the counselor's basic premise was that the individual has sufficient capacity to deal with all those aspects of his life which can come into awareness. So the counselor endeavored to create an interpersonal situation in which material could come into awareness. There was a great deal of stress on both the philosophical and attitudinal characteristics of the therapist, and a definite move away from techniques with perhaps a bit of groping toward a close personal relationship. It was at that time that I began to formulate the three conditions of the therapy which I'll mention a little more fully later on. Then in 1961, when I published *On Becoming a Person,* which contained papers from 1953 to 1960, I had come to recognize quite fully that the therapist must be present as a person in the relationship if therapy is to take place. It is a much more I-Thou kind of relationship that develops between the therapist and the client filled with the same philosophy of not imposing.

EVANS: Martin Buber (1965) used these I-Thou terms earlier. Can you define the terms as they have become most meaningful to you?

ROGERS: I think that some of Buber's phrases would do the best job. When there is a real trendless immediacy in the relationship, when you're aware of nothing but this person and he's aware of nothing but you, and there is a deep sense of communication and unity between the two of you, that's the thing I refer to as I-Thou relationship.

EVANS: Which is in contrast to what?

ROGERS: In contrast to an I-It relationship, where I'm seeing the client as a complex object, a machine whose functions may be in disrepair in certain ways. The whole diagnostic look at an individual is in sharp contrast to the I-Thou kind of relationship.

EVANS: What evolved from this I-Thou relationship, of course, was your idea of the importance of the therapist's compassionate nondirection, rather than direction. In fact, you've been accused of being so nondirective that you wouldn't respond to a client's literal cry for help. Have you undergone any changes yourself in how nondirective or client-centered one can really be? That is, would you say today that you have perhaps qualified somewhat this notion of being nondirective?

ROGERS: No. I think perhaps I enriched it, but not really qualified it. I still feel that the person who should guide the client's life is the client. My whole philosophy and whole approach is to try to strengthen him in that way of being, that he's in charge of his own life and nothing that I say is intended to take that capacity or that opportunity away from him. It is changed in this respect, that I would try to be aware of my own feelings and express them as my feelings without imposing them on him. I would express even negative feelings. I might tell a client, "I'm really bored by what you're saying." It doesn't guide him. It does provide him with some rather jolting data which he must handle in some way or other. But I'm not telling him what he should do to avoid boring me. Maybe he would just as soon bore me; that's up to him.

EVANS: I'm sure you really don't mean it literally, but back when you were working on your 1942 book, would you have actually made this kind of comment to the client?

ROGERS: No, I wouldn't have. At that time, I was quite fascinated by the discovery that people did have much more capacity to guide themselves than I'd given them credit for. I became sort of a tourist in that, thinking "Let's not let any of me into the situation except just an understanding of the client's feelings." I gradually realized over the years that the tourist approach shakes the client out of what might be a very close interpersonal relationship which is more rewarding. I might just say that what really started me in the change from the manipulative approach to one which rested its confidence in the client were a number of experiences. Perhaps the most vivid one is this. I'd been working with a mother, and a lot of the other staff members were working with her son, and I was getting nowhere with this mother. I felt she was a rejecting mother and tried to gently point that out. But we just made no progress. After a number of interviews, I said to her, "I think we've both tried, but I don't think we're getting anywhere, and I suggest that we just call it quits." She agreed that she didn't think that we were getting very far, either. She got up and started to leave the room and got as far as the door, and said, "Do you ever take adults for counseling here?" I said, "Yes." She said, "All right," and came back and sat right down again and began to pour out her own problems from her own point of view, which was totally different from the nice case history I had gotten. I began to really work on things that concerned her, primarily her marriage and not her son at all. That was the start of a really fruitful therapeutic relationship. It made me realize that if I wanted to look like a smart psychologist, I could go ahead and diagnose and advise and interpret. But if I wanted to be effective in working with people, then I might just as well recognize that this person has the capacity to deal with his own problems if I could create a climate where he could do it. Since that time, I would say my whole effort has been focused on the kind of psychological climate that helps the individual to resolve his problems, to develop and to grow.

EVANS: The tendency to focus on the contemporaneous view of the present field of the client is in sharp contrast with the Freudian notion of going back into the patient's history. In this respect, your theories were consistent with Kurt Lewin's notion of field theory, which implies that behavior is a function of the person interacting with his present environment. Were you literally affected by Lewin's work? Were you aware of it?

ROGERS: Not very sharply aware of it. As I became aware of it, I realized certainly that I was operating from a field theory in the sense of analyzing all influences on the individual in the present situation and not from a genetic theory in the sense of analyzing the historical past of the individual.

EVANS: Now, another possible influence would seem to be the work of Otto Rank. Rank, of course, emphasized time setting in the process of therapy. He would say, "Let's finish this up in so many sessions," which might be simply a matter of weeks or months. This is such a contrast from three to five years of prolonged therapy, or the indeterminate length of traditional psychoanalysis. Were you influenced by Rank?

ROGERS: Yes, I was. I was not so much influenced by the setting of a time limit, but by many of his other ideas of the relationship and focusing more on the immediate present. I was influenced primarily in an indirect way. Some people who had worked with the Philadelphia School of Social Work, which was quite Rankian in its orientation, had quite an impact on me and they got Rank to Rochester for a three-day seminar which was fruitful. I have sometimes said facetiously that in those three days I didn't think much of his theory, but I thought his therapy was very good. There's no doubt that my "therapy" was influenced by his thinking.

EVANS: A moment ago you mentioned some of the principles that seemed to guide your thinking about psychotherapy today, and you said that you were interested more in techniques. One technique which you emphasized went hand in hand with your client-centered notion and involved encouraging the therapist to genuinely reflect feeling. Would you still go along with this idea of the importance of genuine reflection?

ROGERS: Let me talk about the conditions that I feel are necessary to therapy, and I think in doing that I'll answer your question. We've gradually built up a fairly solid theory, and backed it up with some pretty satisfactory research which shows that if these conditions are not the ultimate or best statement of what fosters personal growth, they are at least an approximation of it. The existence of these three conditions is very important to the relationship. First, and most important, is therapist congruence or genuineness—his ability to be a real person with the client. Second is the therapist's ability to accept the client as a separate person without judging him or evaluating him. It is rather an unconditional acceptance—that I'm able to accept you as you are. The third condition is a real empathic understanding. That's where the term *reflection* was used. If it is simply reflection, that's no good. That's just a technique. It must be a desire to understand empathically, to really stand in the client's shoes and to see the world from his vantage point. If some of that can be communicated to the client, that I do really see how you feel and understand the way you feel, that can be a most releasing kind of experience. To find that here is a real person who really accepts and understands sensitively and accurately perceives just the way the world seems to me—that just seems to pull people forward. The effect that can have is really fascinating. It is this aspect that enables the process of therapy to go on.

EVANS: In terms of describing this particular relationship between client and counselor, you were in a position where you had to contend with the very powerful construct of transference that Freud had developed. His notion was that the therapist was perceived by his patient as a "parent," reflecting some early relationships with his actual parent, and that positive transference between the therapist and the patient would be a projection of love toward the parent or negative transference would be a projection of hate toward the parent. He also introduced the notion of the therapist's attitude toward the patient as a countertransference, which could also be positive or negative. Freud was apparently trying to say that the therapist should have a sort of affective neutrality. When you emphasize the importance of an unconditional positive regard that the therapist must have for the patient, you certainly are not looking at the unconscious irrational nature of this relationship in the sense of a countertransference, are you?

ROGERS: The interesting thing about Freud's formulation is that, as in so many of his formulations, there is no room for a normal feeling reaction between the two. It's either transference or countertransference, but the possibility of having a "normal feeling of liking toward another person" just doesn't fit into his theory. But I think it's fascinating the way, except among pretty orthodox Freudians, the whole notion of transference and countertransference has pretty well faded out of the picture. I think that the phenomenon of transference as it existed in psychoanalysis was a learned thing, fostered by the reactions of the analyst. We frequently see evidences of transference in therapy where it's clear that the therapist is regarded as the father figure, or in some other way definitely related to the client's past. But we deal with that as we deal with any of his feelings, and by understanding the way it seems to him, the irrational aspects tend to dissolve. For example, a person may be irrationally angry at his employer. As he talks that out, and it's accepted and understood, he can gradually begin to see that part of it isn't reasonable and part of it is reasonable. The irrational things tend to drop away. In the same way, if he looks upon his therapist as: "You're just like my father and so I hate you just the way I hated him"; if he can express that openly and it's accepted and understood, then the irrational aspects tend to dissolve away from that. What remains is whatever his real reaction is to the real person sitting there with him.

EVANS: There has been a tremendous revolution in our whole conception of psychotherapy, and obviously your work has contributed to this. Increasingly we have moved away from individual face-to-face therapy, as you described in your early work, into the area of group therapy where groups of individuals become part of the therapy process. Group therapy is still growing by leaps and bounds. Aside from group therapy as such, variations of group-encounter techniques such as sensitivity training, an outgrowth of the group dynamics orientation, have taken on new importance. Even more broadly, the whole personal growth movement has moved into what we call the encounter group. Group encounter seems to be developing a number of innovations. Dramatic variations, such as nudity among participants, touching, massaging, spiritual and various other transcendental dimensions are becoming a part of group encounters. In other words, in terms of trying to develop this interpersonal encounter you've been talking about, it seems that suddenly the message is: "Yes. Use every technique of communication, tactual, visual or what have you." How do you see yourself in regard to this whole movement?

ROGERS: Let me focus on my encounter-group aspect of it because, as you know, I've completed a book on that (Rogers, 1970), and it's a field in which I'm very much involved. I think that in many ways it can, and, in some respects, has gone completely wild, and I regret that. In its more solid aspects, it's one of the most significant social inventions of this century because it is a way of eliminating alienation and loneliness, of getting people into better communication with one another, of helping them develop fresh insights into themselves, and helping them get feedback from others so that they perceive how they are received by others. It serves a great many useful purposes. In my own work with encounter groups, I have very much the same theory and philosophy that I've been talking about. As a group facilitator, I would try to hold much the same attitudes that I was describing as effective in individual psychotherapy. And one reason for my great interest in encounter groups is that I have seen very positive results from them in a relatively short space of time.

EVANS: What are some of the fears that you have about this movement? Do you think there's some danger that extremist offshoots could actually set the whole movement back?

ROGERS: Yes, I think that's a definite possibility. I don't really object, basically, to people trying various approaches—Zen, mysticism, even nude groups if they want to. The social effect that will have, though, is going to be very bad because I think the general public may get turned off and feel that all groups are bad, just as a number of years ago they got turned off about progressive education, and that became a dirty word. The analogy might be quite close because the public may turn against groups, and yet I'm sure that the kinds of things that an encounter-group experience does for people will continue, just as progressive education as a term is no longer used, but the sound ideas of progressive education have been operating in that field ever since.

EVANS: You're really saying, then, that some of these experimental approaches may have some value, but the extremist views could damage the encounter-group movement seriously?

ROGERS: That's right. It could damage the whole picture of encounter groups in the public eye.

THE FORMAL EDUCATIONAL SYSTEM

PART IV

Overview | Carl Rogers has been particularly interested in the formal educational system in the United States. In this section, we discuss the problems at various levels of the educational system and his particular philosophy of education, including his reaction to the so-called student protest movement of a few years ago.

EVANS: It seems to me that one of the most interesting reflections of your life's work has been your book dealing with education, *Freedom to Learn* (1969). It's a rather bold attempt to look very seriously and very critically at the American educational system. What are some of the deficiencies of the American educational system that led you to write this book?

ROGERS: I don't think I should begin to go into all that. It would be too long a list. I feel that conventional education from primary school through graduate school is probably the most outdated, incompetent, and bureaucratic institution in our culture. It's also pretty much irrelevant to the interests of the students. It's really very disturbing to me. I have three grandchildren in college and I've talked to them as they went through high school and grammar school. Their description of what goes on in education today is almost identical with what it was fifty years ago when I was in school. To me, that's incredible!

There have been such changes in religious institutions, in industry, in every institution you can mention, but education clings to the past like a leech. I think that perhaps it's because, unlike almost every other institution, educators get no feedback from their consumers. They listen to the alumni; they listen to the board of education; they listen to the board of regents; they listen to politicians; but they do not bother to get feedback from their consumers. I think education has become quite out of touch with the modern world.

EVANS: What are some of the specific things that you see in our early elementary or primary grades that trouble you?

ROGERS: There's even research evidence to show that the child's spirit of autonomy, and so on, decreases as he goes through the grammar school experience. He comes out of it less autonomous and less independent. I'm not sure there's research on this, but he also comes out of it less curious than when he entered. He's learned to conform, to say "Yes, ma'am" and "No, ma'am" or "Yes, sir" and "No, sir" to his teachers and to regurgitate their thoughts upon request. I think the primary grades have been perhaps less damaged and less deficient than some of the others because a good many teachers in the primary grades do treat their children like persons, but not all, I must say, not all.

EVANS: Obviously, the thrust of some of your observations is toward secondary schools, junior high school and high school. This is a very tricky period in the life of the individual. He is now moving to the point where he is in a way an adult, while at the same time a child, a teen-ager. The school system inherits this particular problem, this growing individual caught up between the world of the adult and the world of the child. How has our educational system responded to this?

ROGERS: I was trying to think how I could answer that briefly. I think my deepest criticism of the educational system at that period, and that also applies to other periods, is that it's all based upon a distrust of the student. Don't trust him to follow his own leads; guide him; tell him what to do; tell him what he should think; tell him what he should learn. Consequently at the very age when he should be developing adult characteristics of choice and decision making, when he should be trusted on some of those things, trusted to make mistakes and to learn from those mistakes, he is, instead, regimented and shoved into a curriculum, whether it fits him or not.

EVANS: Now, isn't there a very fine line here which is implicit in the "limits of freedom" notion? Let's take a very concrete example. There is a great deal of concern today about sex education in the schools. This has generated many questions concerning where the family and parents' responsibility begins and ends, and where the teachers' and the school system's responsibility begins and ends. How can you resolve this problem? It really reflects the problem of the responsibility for the child's personality growth and development versus the responsibility for the child's intellectual growth and development, doesn't it?

ROGERS: Let me first dwell on another aspect of it. Even the way that whole issue is voiced shows very strongly that it is a concern about what we should teach them. No one thinks of asking the student, "What would you like to learn? What do you need to know about sex? Have you learned enough at home that you're quite satisfied? Would you like other facts and materials?" We start on all the wrong assumptions, that we, the superior beings, must decide what is good for him to learn. I don't go along with that at all.

EVANS: The key to a lot of these problems seems to be finally reflected in the attitudes of the college students. After all this exposure to the educational system in the primary and secondary grades, the college student has arrived at a certain point of maturity. Although not as conspicuous as it was a few years ago, there is still much unrest among these students. Do you believe that some of the student unrest in our universities is due to this restriction of the freedom to learn that characterized much of his earlier education?

ROGERS: Yes, or even more deeply, let me put it this way. If the college student found that his college learning was exciting to him, was relevant, had meaning for him in his everyday life, if he could see a relationship between what he was learning and what he was doing, and was going to do, you couldn't hire students to riot. They would be thrilled by the chance of going on with their learning. I grant that there are many other causes of student unrest, such as war and ecological problems. They might get very restive about these situations, but if their learning was as exciting to them as it should be, and could be, there really would be very little basis for taking it out on the colleges. They might try to take it out on the military establishment, or whatever else they're protesting against. But

I think much of this campus unrest springs from the fact that college has not been a rewarding place for a young person to be, although changes in a more relevant direction are increasingly apparent.

EVANS: Let's go back for a moment to a problem that we have today. Nevitt Sanford (1962) in an earlier book and Arthur Chickering in a more recent book, *Education and Identity* (1969), have looked at this whole problem of relevance and personality development on the college campus. The suggestion might be that the university should be a place to allow for the full development of the individual's personality and provide for an opportunity to become more self-actualized, or whatever term you want to use there. At the same time, we might argue, as you say, that the things we teach the student relating to his intellectual development should be more relevant, that content be more meaningful. But in the final analysis, isn't this whole conception of developing an interest in knowledge for its own sake also a crucial mission of the university? In other words, can't there be something exciting about gaining knowledge in itself? Isn't there a point at which we might almost become anti-intellectual if we were to try to relate everything to either the growth of the student's personality or his immediate adjustment to life?

ROGERS: Yes, this gets back to my own conception of significant learning. That is something that takes place with the whole person. I think that the reason you are seeing a certain amount of anti-intellectualism is that for so long it has been an absolutely integral part of the "Ten Commandments" that learning has nothing to do with you except from the neck up, and that it is a completely intellectual abstract idea. I think young people are finally resisting that. I think it was unsound in the first place, but it had a place when most of your life was lived outside of educational institutions, and your feeling life found expression in other ways. Now that education is such a dominant force in the life of the young person, I think we've got to educate the whole person. Sure, I hope someone will get interested in very esoteric subjects if that's what intrigues him, and follow that clear through. But there ought to be a place, too, for the emotional learnings, for getting to know oneself better as a feeling person.

EVANS: How do you separate a statement like this which has a profound meaning in your work and the work of individuals such as Nevitt Sanford and David Riesman from more superficial writings and pronouncements which give lip service to something like this? How do you separate the substance of this process from the rhetoric?

ROGERS: Again, I would have to say, ask the young people. They know perfectly well when they're getting an education which is far from being an education of the whole person. They know when their learning is completely abstract and intellectual, guided and chosen by someone else. We don't bother to ask them. They are quite right to listen skeptically to the educators who say their aim is to educate the whole person. If you watch their operations, it's not what they're doing at all. The people who know that are the consumers of education—the students.

EVANS: Approaching this point in a different way, let's break down that term, *the whole person,* as it relates to the educational system. Is there room in this system for some abstract intellectuality? Is there some way of making something abstract meaningful, even though it has no immediate relevance to the student?

ROGERS: There's absolutely no question about that. Young people are curious, and, given an opportunity to be curious along lines that appeal to them, surely some of them would go into very abstract material. I think of one teacher I haven't thought of for a long time. He was very, very skeptical about my ideas on education. He told me, "I'm a mathematics teacher and you couldn't possibly teach mathematics that way." I said, "Well, maybe you feel you couldn't; I think it could be taught that way." So he tried it that summer with a group of students who had failed math courses and let them go at their own speed, choose what they were interested in, and so on. They didn't all become expert mathematicians, but some of them got so intrigued by mathematics that two of them worked with him on a paper on a highly abstract mathematical concept which was later published. They got all excited about it and really developed it fully.

EVANS: Suppose you were addressing yourself to the president of a university who very seriously wanted to move toward education of the whole person. Ideally, what are some of the steps he could take to move in that direction—away from the more formal structure to the student-centered structure that you're discussing?

ROGERS: The thing he would be asked to give attention to, first of all, is the attitude of the faculty, because conventional education is entrenched in faculty minds and attitudes. He should either choose a new faculty that has reasonable attitudes toward persons, or he should try to get faculty and students to think together. This is the approach we took in our project in the Immaculate Heart College, where we had faculty and students together in encounter groups. The faculty learned how they were perceived by the students and vice versa. They learned to communicate as people, not as a faculty member up here and a student down there. It really induced a remarkable change in a good many of the faculty members.

EVANS: As we found in our work on *Resistance to Innovation in Higher Education* (Evans, 1968), the faculty member has a special stake in the status quo and resists this sort of thing. Isn't the very nature of training the so-called content specialist, that whole process involved in attaining the Ph.D., likely to increase the probability that this person won't be able to function in the kind of ideal university that you're talking about? Is it realistic to believe that you could go into one of our large state universities with perhaps one or two thousand faculty members and really make some important inroad? Of course, they have worked a little on this problem in certain experimental colleges, but they continue to be just that—experimental. They even continue to call them "experimental" colleges, because the term *experimental* implies that the program may not be adopted generally.

ROGERS: I'm not too optimistic on that. I think that

theoretically it could be done, but I'm not very optimistic that it will be done. I think that perhaps what is going to happen—and this is a thought I wouldn't have entertained at all ten years ago—is that education may move outside of our universities. This seems unthinkable to us today. But when you think of another great institution, the church, most significant religious experience has moved outside of the conventional church at the present time. I believe you could find many people who would agree with that. In the same way, I think that we may still have the great buildings, the great campuses, but that really significant learning will be what goes on outside of those. For example, when I was consulting with Cal Tech, they became really concerned because of their dropouts at the end of the freshman year. Who was dropping out? Well, a few of the poor students were dropping out, though they don't get many poor ones there. What really troubled them was that some of the greatest, most creative students were saying, "I don't want any more of this. I'm leaving." This is a small sign in the wind, but students are saying, "I'm not going to take much more of this. I'd rather do my learning outside."

EVANS: Looking at this in a very grim and cynical way, does this mean that we're really seeing the beginning of the end of the American university as we know it? Are you that fearful?

ROGERS: I think that unless the university really wakes up and makes drastic change in itself, that we are seeing not necessarily the beginning of the end—I'm sure that it will continue just as the churches have continued—but the beginning of the end of its major significance in American life. I don't think I've ever said anything quite that extreme before so I probably should qualify it a little bit. Young people are not going to put up with a rigid institution. This is one thing that is exceedingly clear, and most educational institutions are certainly rigid.

EVANS: If we look at this kind of shell of the university that you're describing, what are its functions? Taking our analogy with the church a little further, what would the university be doing then? Would you say it would cease to attract the more creative individual and become a kind of technical training center? Would it lose most of its penchant for the creative and the innovative?

ROGERS: You're trying to get me to gaze very deeply into the crystal ball, and I don't know if I'm that adept at it. Yes, I think it might cease to be the source of really creative thinking in our culture. I sometimes wonder whether that isn't almost true at the present time.

EVANS: Suppose you were to hear that one of your grandchildren was dropping out of college for the same reason as the Cal Tech students. Your three grandchildren are, I understand, very bright and creative young people. What would your reaction be? Would you be inclined to say, "Well, I understand this, and I hope that they grow beyond this . . . ?

ROGERS: It's not hypothetical. Two of them have dropped out. Both are going back this fall, but I think it was a very constructive thing in both instances. They dropped out temporarily for quite different reasons, but part of it was disillusionment with the system.

EVANS: Kenneth Kenniston (1967), in his very interesting early work on student unrest, confirmed some of the things you've said about the so-called student protesters. In general, he finds they do come from progressive family structures, are intelligent, and tend to be very bright, superior students. We're not necessarily talking about that extreme radical element that was probably engaged in disruption for its own sake, but about the rank-and-file students that were protesting. If we find this becoming a kind of snowball, we'll find more and more of these people leaving the university and looking elsewhere to learn. What about the stake that the so-called establishment, or society in general, has in the production of physicians and lawyers, and other more specific professions, much less the creative arts and other forms of liberal education?

ROGERS: I'd just as soon limit my remarks to physicians for a moment, because I do know a little about the training of physicians. I think that medical schools are perhaps more aware than liberal arts colleges of some of these problems. They're trying very hard to revise their curriculum to make it more student-centered, to give students a participant part in choosing their curriculum. If they can change, we will continue to have physicians. If a medical school holds to the "good old" model, it may find it is losing students.

EVANS: Of course, your own son is a dean of a medical school, and you undoubtedly discuss this problem with him. There are those who would argue that the medical school or some of the professional schools are the last to catch up with these trends, that they're much more locked into tight, rigid curricula and may be the first to perish.

ROGERS: I'm sure I get a somewhat biased view of that situation through my son, but I think the medical schools that I happen to be close to—the ones here and Johns Hopkins—are really in the forefront of trying to change medical education. I'm not as pessimistic about that as I am, for example, about the training of psychologists. The medical school has such a specific task to do that it is terribly important to both the faculty and the students that students catch on fire from their training and really learn to become good physicians. If they're not achieving that, they get feedback of no uncertain sorts.

PART V

ISSUES IN CONTEMPORARY PSYCHOLOGY

Training of Psychologists

A New Philosophy of Science for Psychology

Interdisciplinary Cooperation Through Personal Encounter

Overview | Carl Rogers has in recent years been particularly interested in various issues in contemporary psychology. In this section, we discuss the way in which he believes professional psychologists should be trained. We also discuss his conception of a new philosophy of science for psychology. Finally, we discuss interdisciplinary cooperation through the personal-encounter technique.

EVANS: Earlier, we briefly discussed training in psychology. The area of clinical psychology obviously is undergoing extremely serious reexamination. There is a great deal of talk today about what we call community psychology. Some are calling clinical psychology applied social psychology, and saying that the idea of training psychologists to administer Rorschach tests and engage in face-to-face psychotherapy belongs to the past. We've got to look at entirely new dimensions. Do you agree that this is a trend?

ROGERS: Yes, I think so. You'd probably be surprised to know how relatively remote I am right now from the training of clinical psychologists, but from my fairly limited vantage point, I see two trends. One is toward a much broader application of psychological principles in interpersonal relationships to groups, and to community problems. The other trend is toward establishing separate professional schools for the training of clinical psychologists. That probably makes sense. I used to be opposed to that and felt we should hold academic psychology and clinical psychology together as long as possible because they would interact fruitfully with each other.

EVANS: This, of course, is just one area. What's happening to the rest of psychology? We might move clinical to one side, but we still have the so-called scientific discipline of psychology. There is probably more student interest in majoring in this field than ever before in history, and it appears that society's interest in employing psychologists is going to continue to increase. What are we going to do? What are some of the changes you would make in graduate training if you were to direct curriculum reexamination for a graduate program in psychology in all fields?

ROGERS: First of all I would involve the graduate students in a very responsible way, in helping to devise what should be done. It's always been my opinion that if you really want to know a graduate school or a graduate faculty, ask the graduate students. They know, and I think that they could be helpful in devising a better approach to some of these things. I'm ambivalent as to the training of professionals. I think it's fine if clinical psychologists and the rest of psychology can be held together. If not, then perhaps social psychologists who expect to work in the community should have separate programs, maybe along with the clinicians. Another solution might be to have a whole school of applied psychology as well as the more academic approach.

EVANS: What would make up the unified body of

knowledge that people would be required to have in order to function in the field of psychology? For example, we do stress research, statistics, and experimental design. We talk about learning theory, cognition and perception, personality theory, and history of psychology. These things are all a general input. What should we be producing? Should we stress rigorous training of researchers during this period when we're surrounded by chaos in our environment?

ROGERS: I think there is much room for a strong emphasis on the applied fields. Psychology is probably too focused at the present time on the training of researchers, but I'd hate to see that go down the drain. I'd rather see a new philosophy of science in psychology. That's another topic, though. To get back to what I'd do if I were in charge of a graduate program, I suspect I would supply plenty of real applied training along with whatever is central to the field. Now, you say what would be that central field? It may not be unified anymore. We may have grown to the point where psychology is just a label that covers quite diverse things, just as medicine covers everything from bacteriology to computer science to heart specialists. I don't think we should struggle too hard to find a unity which may not, in fact, be there. There are many legitimate interests in the psychological realm, and a good graduate department should have lots of diversity in following those different fields of knowledge.

EVANS: You alluded to what seems to me to be an extremely important aspect of our discussion of contemporary problems in psychology—the need for developing a new philosophy of science for psychology. What do you mean by this?

ROGERS: I think it's quite clear that psychology is very much tied to the Newtonian concepts of science which were borrowed from physics. That whole conception is quite out of date in physics at the present time, and it is even more inappropriate in the field of psychology. I'm not quite certain what the new science should be, but I don't think it will do away with the rigorous empiricism that we've always known. Empiricism will remain a part of our science, but for large areas of psychological knowledge, we need a much more human science. I'm not sure what form that may take, but I think it will not be far from phenomenological. We will stop trying to look entirely at persons from the outside, and begin to try to understand the individual's own phenomenal world. I believe that it is possible to do good empirical studies based upon phenomenological data. We also need more stress on naturalistic observation. I feel that psychology has endeavored to jump so far into science in order to be comparable to physics that it has become in many aspects a scientism. I don't believe that we're confronting the most fundamental problems of the human condition. Instead, we study only what we can measure, and I don't like that. I feel that a real scientist tackles the problems that are most significant in his area of interest. We may have to crawl before we can walk. We may have to do close naturalistic study before we can begin to do more empirical studies.

EVANS: One of the most important current challenges to psychology, which will probably continue for many years to come, is the fact that we are surrounded by really serious problems, such as air pollution. It's clear that these are not the kinds of problems with which a particular discipline can deal by itself. The engineer, the chemist, or the physician interested in the area of public health cannot solve the pollution problem by himself. It's obvious that solving this problem will require a crossing of disciplines. In our earlier discussion on the university, we might have continued to point out what you're implying—not only that professors are rather rigidly pigeonholing themselves into little boxes, but they are parts of individual departments which tend to do this. This is true of all disciplines. If the government wishes to encourage the crossing of disciplines in addressing itself to these really crucial problems that may challenge our very survival, how would it go about doing so? What can be done to break down these barriers? Even psychologists and sociologists with very closely related perspectives often can't work together.

ROGERS: I know of situations where they've housed members of different disciplines in the same building, hoping that somehow they will cross-fertilize each other's thinking. That just doesn't happen. When a group of individuals from different disciplines are faced with the solution of a specific problem, they find they can communicate with each other, and they start to tackle the problem. Of course, that doesn't resolve the whole thing; it doesn't change the attitudes of some of the people involved. They may be very frightened of moving out of their little boxes. It would help, however, and I do feel that task or problem orientation is the thing that will bring scientists together. It would be a great thing if the government would give money, for the time being only, for such interdisciplinary projects because psychologists have a great deal to learn from contact with the world and with other disciplines.

EVANS: Could some of the encounter-group methods be used to get a group of so-called content specialists to work together?

ROGERS: There's no question but that encounter groups, or team-building groups, which are a variation of encounter groups, would be of considerable help. There's plenty of evidence from industry that this method works. The space industry, for example, has faced this same problem. How do you get engineers, electronics people, and people in very highly specialized areas to work together to produce one complex space product? They've found they are almost forced to use an encounter type of method that improves communication and interpersonal relationships to produce a team that will work together. It is easier to get a group of people in business to communicate than it is to get a group of academic people to communicate, although I don't regard it as a hopeless task, particularly if developing communication skills, per se, became a condition of work. For example, if you wanted to join this team to work on pollution, you would have to be willing to become involved in several encounter-type groups. Then you would get results.

EVANS: The tricky thing is that this goes back to

the whole problem of encounter groups we discussed earlier. Academic people developed such a negative image of encounter groups that the very concept has become a source of resistance when you're trying to get a group of people to work toward some constructive goal. What strategy could be used to overcome this? Let's say that the National Science Foundation was currently anxious to support creative efforts, across interdisciplinary lines, to deal with ecological problems such as pollution. What advice would you give to one of the staff members of the foundation eager to get interdisciplinary efforts started?

ROGERS: Two strategies would be necessary. One of the reasons academic people especially are afraid of encounter groups is that they sound personal, and they're terribly afraid of being personal with anybody. I would drop any emphasis on the personal side of it and make it a communications group or a team-building group, or something like that. In other words, the more it is focused on the task to be done, the more acceptable it is to the academic person. The executive council of a college that we worked with became a task-oriented group and considered how the college could be improved. People from different disciplines were on the executive council. When we interviewed them to find out what problems they had, some of the problems were definitely personal. We brought up those personal problems as well as the others, but it was done in the context of dealing with the task to be accomplished.

EVANS: Could you develop this point further, since

this problem of working toward an abstract goal versus a personal problem is central to the success of interdisciplinary problems?

ROGERS: I'd say that most so-called abstract goals of groups seem less personal and yet turn out to have a definite personal value. If you and I are supposed to work together on a task and we begin to analyze why we aren't doing very well in working together on it, some of that will be straight and factual stuff. Maybe one or the other of us is lacking in knowledge we need to complete the task by himself. Some of it will be interpersonal, as some of the things you do get on my nerves and vice versa. So, it's in working out those elements too that progress would be made.

EVANS: Would you go so far as to say that if the National Institutes of Health or the National Science Foundation, or, for that matter, any of the groups that are trying to deal with global problems, started with this premise, that such a team-building approach should probably be built into the legislation or the directives that implement these interdisciplinary programs? Would you consider it that important?

ROGERS: Yes. Directives are the conditions under which the grant is made and should include a professionally developed team-building effort.

EVANS: When you say "professionally developed," would you say that they could conceivably be a team of consultants? For example, let's say University X, working with the community, is about to embark on solving a serious problem of water pollution, or the problem of developing a mass transportation system. As the first step, should this university and community group bring in an outside expert in this type of team-building as part of the protocol? In fact, should this effort automatically begin with the assistance of such a team-building professional?

ROGERS: Yes, that is the way to go about it. You're right in suggesting an outside consultant, because it's a little hard to serve as a consultant from inside the group. For some reason, it's easier to take an outside consultant and also easier to criticize him, and that's healthy, too.

PART VI

RETROSPECT AND PROSPECT

Psychologist's Role in Solving Social Problems

Existentialism, Humanism, Free Will, and Determinism

The Declining Importance of Psychoanalytic Theory

The Medical Model and Psychology

Limitations of Classification of Mental Disorders

Views on Community Psychiatry and Psychology

Situational Ethics and the "Generation Gap"

Pornography, Drugs, and Violence

Important Influences on His Work

Estimate of His Own Most Important Contributions

Reactions to Critics and Criticism

Plans for the Future

Overview | In this section, our discussion ranges over a variety of topics. We discuss the problem of what the psychologist's role should be in solving social problems. The philosophical issues of existentialism, humanism, and free will versus determinism are explored. Also discussed are the declining importance of psychoanalytic theory, the possible adverse effects of applying the medical model to psychological practice, and the limitations of the formal classification of mental disorders in the diagnosis of mental illness. Dr. Rogers also has an opportunity to react to the community psychiatry and psychology movement, the role of situational ethics in the so-called generation gap, and pornography, drugs, and violence in our culture. Finally, in a more personal vein, Dr. Rogers responds to questions concerning what he considers to be his most important contributions, criticisms of his work, and his plans for the future.

EVANS: Dr. Rogers, suppose that today you were President of the American Psychological Association, just as you were some years ago, and you were sitting down to write your presidential address. What would be some of the things you would include? It probably would be a little different address from the one you gave some years ago, wouldn't it?

ROGERS: Yes, it would. That's a really difficult question because, traditionally, the president speaks about his own work, and I'm not sure I'd want to do that. If I spoke about the problems of the profession, one of my deepest concerns would be the remoteness of the psychological profession from the live social issues that exist today. Another concern regards the exceedingly sterile graduate training we give to psychologists. We stifle a great deal of creative thought in the way we train persons in the psychological profession.

EVANS: The very fact that you would make a new address so different from your previous presidential addresses, which dealt with your research, is intriguing. Doesn't that say something about the changing perspective for psychology as well as the manner in which you yourself have changed?

ROGERS: I guess it does say something about me and about the profession. I am really concerned about the directions in which psychology as a profession is going.

EVANS: I recall a conversation that I had with Sir Julian Huxley in London a few years ago, which suggested something that's both challenging and disturbing to the behavioral sciences. He used a thermometer analogy. He pointed out how our world is increasingly jeopardized by problems such as pollution and the possibility of nuclear war for which solutions will depend largely on knowledge of human relations. Our knowledge of the technology which created these problems registers high up on the thermometer. Our knowledge of human relations necessary to solve these problems barely registers above zero on that thermometer. Do you share his pessimism? Is the gap between potentially destructive technical knowledge and knowledge of human relations too wide to resolve?

ROGERS: I have a great deal of confidence in man's potential for resolving his own problems. This grows out of my experience in therapy and in groups. But that confidence is based on the condition that the person is really aware of the facts. For example, in therapy, he becomes more and more aware of the inner facts about himself. In groups he becomes more aware of his relationships in communication with others as well as developing fresh insights into himself. When he is in possession of all the psychological facts, he is profoundly capable of mastering whatever problems face him. I have somewhat the same confidence in man in his social groupings. What really troubles me about today's society is too little awareness of all the facts. I feel that a great many people—politicians, government officials, industry, extreme right wing, extreme left wing—are all in the business of concealing facts. I don't know if man will have the facts available to him to make sensible and sound decisions in this very crucial period. Someone asked me not long ago if I was an optimist or a pessimist in regard to mankind. I responded that I had enormous confidence in the individual, and in the small group, but for the reasons I've given, my attitude toward the future of our culture is that we're on a knife-edge balance. I don't know whether we will make it or not. If there should be, say, a right-wing take-over—which I regard as probably much more likely than a left-wing take-over—psychologists would have a great deal to contribute to anyone who took over the dictatorship. Psychologists have prided themselves in predicting and controlling behavior; they could instruct a dictator in manipulating public opinion and molding behavior. They could advise him about the most effective types of propaganda and how to create certain images of people in situations. When you try to figure out the contributions of psychology or the behavioral sciences to a viable democracy, that is a much more difficult thing. There are really only a few psychologists who have contributed ideas that help to set people free, making them psychologically free and self-responsible, encouraging them in decision making and problem solving. I'm especially disappointed in the academic psychologists in the great universities. In the smaller colleges and some of the more outlying places, you find some exciting things going on that are really relevant to our society, but in the great universities, so called, there are very few psychologists who are contributing significantly to the incredible social issues emerging today.

EVANS: One thing you said reminds me of some remarks made by Professor Harold Lasswell (1970) before the American Psychological Association. He said that too often we in the behavioral sciences have become subservient to the leadership, and that we should declare some kind of independence. You're agreeing with him that the danger lies in simply succumbing to whomever is in power, in playing the game without committing ourselves independently.

ROGERS: I'm very much afraid that's exactly what could happen. I see very little in the way of social thinking or social purpose on the part of the behavioral scientists in the universities. I do distinguish that again because outside of the universities I find a great many people in the behavioral sciences who are concerned about social problems and are making a contribution to some of these issues, such as racial problems.

EVANS: Speaking of the racial problem and the apparent progress since Brown *vs.* the Board of Education in 1954, there are those who say, rather cynically, that in the final analysis the real change agents were theologians or people following theological movements. They say that although the behavioral scientists studied this problem of racial prejudice for many years, they actually contributed very little to changes toward equality. Do you agree with this?

ROGERS: Yes, I would, but I'm glad that there are a few exceptions. Men like Kenneth Clark and some others that I know have made real contributions, but their number is very small. I think it goes back to a rather fundamental lack in psychologists—that it is not in fashion to believe anything. Of course, a scientist must be a skeptical person, willing to disavow findings that are not solid, willing to look skeptically at new discoveries. In my estimation, there is also a place for real conviction. I feel it's a part of a general picture of academic psychology to be overtly concerned with being scientific, but if you ask them what they believe, what convictions they hold, they say, "Oh, not any." They feel that would be unscientific. This incredibly narrow view of what constitutes a science is one of the things that keeps psychology from being socially significant.

EVANS: Hayek (1956) used the sarcastic term *scientism* to describe this, and you used the term earlier. Are you saying that behavioral scientists have been smothered by *scientism?*

ROGERS: I think they have. As I mentioned earlier, I was very much educated by being a consultant for three years for Cal Tech on some of their educational and human problems. That brought me in touch with a faculty group which included Nobel Prize winners and a couple that I'm sure will be future Nobel Prize winners. To see real scientists, if I may use that phrase, scientists who are imaginative and curious and willing to dream, full of convictions and willing to test their hypotheses and to be proven wrong—in contrast, the constricted scientist in the behavioral field is very depressing. Regarding my own profession, it's very exciting to be in contact with people like that. For example, there's one man who had made tremendous contributions to theoretical physics who felt that he was probably beyond his prime. He was in his thirties, and after all, what physicist makes any contributions beyond the middle thirties? He was seriously thinking of turning to psychology, and I said that I hoped he would. Since then he's definitely changed his mind; he's getting a lot of recognition in physics. When I said to him, "What would you want to go into if you did turn to psychology?" "Well, naturally," he said, "I'd rather go into the areas where the mystery is greatest. Wouldn't that perhaps be the unconscious and hypnotism?" So different from what the ordinary psychologist thinks—he shies away from anything mysterious.

EVANS: Let's go back to the original question—whether the behavioral scientist will learn enough to stop us from being destroyed. You're saying that one of the problems is the very lack of commitment of the psychologist. You're almost saying that he's hiding behind science.

ROGERS: That's right. I feel it's so true that it hurts. He is clearly rejecting the possibility of trying to build a science as other sciences have been built, through careful naturalistic observations first, then more and more refined approaches to the problem. One leap will make it into the minutely refined methodology of an advanced science, and in his heart of hearts, I think he knows he doesn't belong there. Psychology is not that far advanced, so he's an insecure scientist who does have more of a scientism than does a true science. And I like your word, *commitment,* because I think that's probably better than my use of *belief* or *conviction.* He isn't particularly committed to any social view of man or man's problems. He's fearful of doing anything that would really look into the mysteries of the human condition. He wants to just stick to the things he's sure he can measure, and measure exactly.

EVANS: The matter of commitment leads to another general area that might be interesting to discuss. From the very start, your work has been related to the existentialist movement and to the humanist movement. Would it be possible to historically relate the kind of existentialism emerging from Europe during the period when you were first writing in the 1940s, to the kind of thing that has evolved since? One would have thought that you were directly touched by some of the existentialist and humanist philosophers. Did you sit down one day and read Kierkegaard and the other existential thinkers and say, "Ah ha! This is where I should be going"?

ROGERS: That constitutes an interesting story. I can sum it up by saying that once when I was asked to give a talk on existentialism, or existential psychology, I thought that the title of my talk really should be, "How to Become an Existentialist Without Really Trying." The secret is this: in my work, in psychotherapy, I became more and more involved with the present moment, with the choices clients were making, with trying to help an individual create his own life and his own future. I began to think in a great many existentialist terms when I was at the University of Chicago. Some of the theological students there who were taking work with me said they wanted me to read Kierkegaard and Buber. At one time, on an extended Mexican vacation, I had read a lot of Kierkegaard and Buber, but my reaction was a little different from what you say—"Ah ha." It was also the feeling, "My gosh, here are friends of mine that I never knew I had. Here are people who discovered the same sort of things I have, who have gone beyond what I've gone through in a number of significant ways." But, I didn't feel at all as though I was being introduced to a new field. I felt I had been over a lot of this ground myself. My feeling was that it's very pleasant to find that there are friends here that I never knew I had.

EVANS: Certainly much of the French existentialism has been beset by a kind of cynicism. This existentialist philosophy really says man's predicament is almost hopeless, a state of despair. On the other hand, there seems to be a kind of American existentialism which seems to be a good deal more optimistic. You would certainly have to be considered as typical of these American existentialists.

ROGERS: Indeed, I'm not very congenial with the somewhat despairing existentialists, particularly those in France. I have felt closer to existentialists like Kierkegaard and Buber, who, though not unmindful of problems like death and despair, nevertheless take a fundamentally positive view. Just as you say, in this country there is a flavor of existentialism developing which is definitely positive in its view of man, and I certainly would have to place myself there. I think that this positive view could be due to the fact that we've been far more fortunate in our lives. We have not been direct victims of two world wars. We have less reason to be acquainted with despair, so I'm sure of cultural factors entering in here. Nonetheless, I feel that there is a more positive part of existentialism developing in this country.

EVANS: Moving to a slightly different area, to what degree do you believe an important creative effort can or should be separated from the personality of the creator? Freud is an example. People keep seeing everything that Freud wrote as being a problem in his own personal life. But playwright Arthur Miller, in my dialogue with him (Evans, 1969b), indicated that a man's personal life is irrelevant to the understanding of his contribution; ultimately a man's creative contribution must be regarded on its own. Of course, that's not the way many psychologists would think.

ROGERS: No, because the average psychologist is very analytical, which is both a blessing and a curse.

EVANS: How do you feel your own personality is related to your creative ideas in psychology?

ROGERS: I've said sometimes that my generally optimistic point of view could be glandular; I don't know. One facet of this certainly is true—there's no doubt that my interest in growth is positive. I've always been interested even in growth of animals and plants. I spent a good portion of my adolescence on a farm. I've always done some gardening. Here in southern

California, I can garden the year around and I do, and enjoy it. It's not just casual gardening. I said to my wife one day, "What's happened to those two blooms on the white camellia?" And she said, "Don't tell me you keep track of every blossom." I said, "Of course I do." I do have a strong interest in growing things, and I think that people who have this always tend to be realists. You know that y work very hard and it can all go for naught. But on the other hand, you are also involved in what is essentially a living, developing process, and this, of course, has been the keynote of my work with people, too, as I'm interested in growing people. This has been true in therapy, and it's been true with the staff groups I've worked with. I think the thing that I pride myself on most in working with students and patients is that frequently I've been able to help them to grow and develop.

EVANS: This is very interesting because we might interpret your faith in the process of growth and say that it is all part of your humanistic philosophy or a humanistic religion with overtones of an optimistic existentialism. This introduces the problem of the difficulty in coming up with a viable faith or religion that can somehow involve people who want to reconcile the mysticism in most religions with their humanistic elements. In the history of many religions, the fundamentalism, the mysticism, and fear dominated the humanistic values which were also parts of these religions. Can you see transitions or changes in the fundamentalists as they begin to be exposed to the type of humanism espoused in your work?

ROGERS: I differ a little with one assumption which implies that underneath the fundamentalist's point of view there is really a humanism. Now, I'm not so sure there always is. In a deeply defended person—and I would regard the orthodox fundamentalist as being that—change is difficult to bring about. I don't expect a great deal of change. Change tends to occur more in the person who is already somewhat open-minded and searching in his approach to life. I have thoroughly enjoyed all my adult contacts, and I do separate those from childhood contacts with religious figures and religious people. I am very pleased that I spent two years at Union Theological Seminary. That was the best philosophical training I could have gotten anywhere, and I have enjoyed contacts with theological students, with Catholic priests, the whole gamut. On the whole, exposure to humanistic psychology has probably been very good for theologians. When I was at Chicago, theological students who worked as counselors in the counseling center sometimes said to me, "You know, now I begin to understand what religion is all about." They had found something in deep interpersonal relationships that showed them the importance of caring, the significance of understanding, or acceptance—terms they had been using theologically, but that now came to life. I am pleased by that. Once a group of priests who were trying to pin me down asked, "Well, you really are religious, aren't you?" I finally came up with a statement that I think I would stand by, although it's a little paradoxical. I said, "I'm too religious to be religious." To me that statement has some meaning. I did hear a lot about ethical things and moral preference and so on, but I have very little use for the institution of religion or for religious institutions.

EVANS: There are those who argue that Sunday schools or most religious teachings as a means of humanizing man are pretty much a failure because they do not separate the fundamentalist positions with their high fear and mystical components from the more humanistic components.

ROGERS: They probably are too often futile, as they stand. Let me turn away from that a little to something that's related to it. The more I have worked with people, both in individual therapy and in encounter groups, the more respect I've come to have for man as a person worthy of respect and a person of dignity. This value that I've come to place on the human being is something that really grows out of my experience. I didn't start with that high a regard for the individual person. That's probably one of the things that these theological students meant when they felt they had come in contact with deeper values than they had previously experienced in their religious training.

EVANS: Related to this is the renewed interest in the free will versus determinism issue generated by B. F. Skinner's book, *Beyond Freedom and Dignity* (1971). Individuals argue that Skinner undermines the self-deterministic notion that man has a will and is ultimately responsible for control over his own destiny. Skinner, they say, posits an ultimate social-environmental determinism which says that man is almost completely shaped by his environment. Freud and the biologists who influenced him, and many biologists today, continue to hold the genetic-deterministic belief, that man is a product of his genetic capability, that in spite of all other influences the biological makeup of man ultimately controls him. Of course, in psychology, we are inclined to conclude that all these factors converge in the individual. There is built into our value system as psychologists the notion that one of these, social-environmental determinism, is more important than self-determinism and genetic determinism. It's a tough problem for the average psychology student since he is led to believe that science should be value free. How do you resolve this determinism issue?

ROGERS: I suppose I would say that I am not an extremist along those lines, but it's true that I focus on the self-deterministic, rather than social-environmental or genetic-deterministic values in my training of students. I'll try to explain what I mean. There is no doubt that our genetic inheritance sets certain limits on what an individual is going to be and become. Those limits are more capable of being stretched than we had supposed, but there are limits. There's no question in my mind that we are very much shaped by what happens to us in our childhood, in our family life, and in our contact with society. You only have to think of what ghetto living does to an individual to realize what course he's been shaped by to a considerable extent. But then there is also the fact that, in the present moment, it is the person himself who is able to understand those factors that have contributed to who he is, and to choose his own future. I remember one client who really summed it up very beautifully. He had been talking about how his life had been ruined by things that had happened to his family and various circumstances of his previous living. After a long pause he said, "Now that I see all that, I guess it's really up to me." I think that puts the whole thing in a nutshell. Once you're aware of the fact that, "Yes, I've been warped by this; I've been molded by that, and genetically I realize aspects of my own situation. I'm genetically a high-strung person. I can easily get overstimulated. I won't be able to change that, I don't think, by anything I could do. I can live with it in better ways." I think as the person becomes aware of these various factors in his background, he can make realistic and sensible choices as to how he's going to both live with and transcend the circumstances of the past. There are various ways of handling this philosophically. I don't believe in free will in the sense that a person's free to do anything, but to deny the reality of the significance of choice as the strict behaviorists do is totally unrealistic. I think that is a fad which will be shown to be mistaken and that the person can and does choose significantly. I've always been rather pleased that our researchers in psychotherapy have shown that the element that probably changes most in individual therapy is the person's concept of himself. He moves toward being a more confident self, more acceptant of himself; self-hatred decreases. As a person feels genuinely confident of who he is and what he's capable of doing, he goes ahead to utilize his past, his conditioning, and the biological basis of his being in more constructive ways.

EVANS: In the last fifteen years, particularly, there seems to be seeping into society at large the notion, advocated primarily by social scientists in the past, that the criminal and the ghetto dweller are products of deprived environments. The so-called war on poverty of a few years ago seemed to be founded on the socially deterministic premise that if we change the social environment of the individual, he will not become a criminal or societal misfit. Suddenly such a theory becomes a rationalization. In the movie *West Side Story,* in the Officer Krupke song, the juvenile delinquents were telling us they were not responsible for their problems, society was. What happens in a society if its unconstructive members begin to rationalize their behavior in terms of a naïve social-deterministic philosophy? Even today's law enforcement officers often sound like some of the earlier sociology textbooks which posited such a notion of determinism.

ROGERS: I agree that it is a rationalization and that it is an unfortunate one. That's why I feel that you can't just sit back and allow the client to say, "Well, I'm just a product of what society has made me," "I'm a rejecting mother," or whatever. We have evidence to back that up in two studies which have always been of great interest to me. Bill Kell took the records of seventy-five delinquents, used in earlier studies, knowing nothing of their present behavior. He analyzed them very carefully and weighted the various factors that had entered into their behavior, ranging from a healthy family environment to a very pathological kind of environment—a very delinquency-producing kind of environment. The neighborhood, the educational element, physical factors, and several more factors were included. He really tried to make a complete evaluation of different elements that might have affected the child's behavior. We later added one more factor—the individual's understanding of himself, including his realistic or unrealistic perception of himself in relation to his environment. He checked up on the current behavior of those delinquents, and some had become delinquents again. To our amazement and disbelief, the self-understanding factor correlated in the .80s with current behavior, and a thing like family environment, which we had thought would come out at the top, was somewhere in the .30s. Actually, it was so shocking to us at the time of the original study—this was many years ago—that we frankly didn't believe the findings. We laid it on the shelf and later Helen McNeil replicated the same study with another group of seventy-five delinquents and found her correlations weren't quite so high. The ratings weren't quite as well done, but the order of the ratings was still the same, as self-understanding correlated most highly with later behavior. We again were so skeptical that we did a subanalysis. We took delinquents who had never been removed from their own home—they hadn't been sent to a school or placed in a foster home—where the home environment was very bad. We felt that this would really show that the family is the more important factor. Again, self-understanding, even in those delinquents that had to remain in a known bad situation, correlated more highly with their behavior. So the essence of that seemed to be that the person who is realistic about himself, who has a pretty good comprehension of what he's up against, and what factors have influenced his behavior, has a much better chance of controlling his behavior. He can make choices. At the time I didn't appreciate the full depth of that study. It's taken a good many years for me to realize that our findings were more significant than I thought at the time.

EVANS: In this same area, some of us who have worked with the President's Committee on Youth, Crime and Delinquency conducted large community studies. We found that as a social agency supported a deprived family, this support led to greater dependency on the agency, and then to resentment toward the agency. This seems to characterize many of the social welfare programs. We began to realize that what was really lacking in this whole system, which might break into this cycle, were techniques of training people to help themselves and become less dependent. This is consistent with what you're saying. It is extremely hard to get social agencies to react to this because they are locked into an almost naïve system of social determinism which focuses on changing the environment rather than the individual. Have you felt somewhat the same way about these various poverty programs?

ROGERS: Yes, they are really more often failures than successes. A lot of my early professional work was very closely related to the work of social agencies. Some of the work they did was very good, but I felt that particularly those that were more welfare-oriented were pretty much wasting their time. The only thing that really counts is whether you help to develop independence and self-understanding in people. I don't want people to starve—I don't want to be misunderstood on that. They should have means for a way to live, but as far as social rehabilitation is concerned, welfare money isn't what will do it. Another relevant example is the work of the late Fred Stoller at Camarillo State Hospital. Through encounter groups, he met some patients who were judged by the other patients in the group to be ready to leave the hospital. They each had at least two hundred dollars with which to make a start. Working with Stoller, they role-played getting a job, dealing with others, and finding a place to live. They really role-played the whole situation they would be up against after they left. Another group he observed was simply told, "Now, if you get into difficulty, and you can't make it on the outside, come back. You can always have a spot here in the hospital." I've forgotten the percentage, but a great majority of the role-playing group stayed out. This was of great interest to the social agencies and rehabilitation agencies. When the second group tried it without the special treatment the first group received, their recidivism rate was much higher. Not nearly as many managed to stay out because there was someone on whom they could depend and they didn't have to be independent, choosing, deciding people.

EVANS: It's interesting to note that many of the strong conservatives such as William Buckley and Ayn Rand also talk about this need for individuality and individualism. On this count, they would probably agree with what you say about individuality. In fact, left and right groups ideologically would agree with many of the things you're saying. This is an interesting bridge between many liberals and conservatives on the current scene. Individuality and the need to encourage it isn't anyone's particular bailiwick any longer. Obviously, you've observed this.

ROGERS: Yes, I've thought about this and I think the stress on individual independence is something on which you would get a certain amount of agreement from the right wing as well as from the left. I think that too many of our social programs, no matter how well-intentioned they are, tend to overlook individual freedom. There's quite a bit of lip service given to helping people to help themselves. When you come right down to it, there is very little in the way of technique that has been developed for helping persons achieve that independence. That's where perhaps I've gone further than some people in really working with people in such a way that their own self-responsibility has developed.

EVANS: Suppose the government, with the same kind of crash program used to approach the so-called war on poverty, recognized what you're saying and developed a crash program to search for means of getting people to help themselves, to develop new ways of trying to instill this independence on a group basis. How fruitful would this be? To be more concrete, say you were asked by the current Secretary of Health, Education and Welfare, "Would it be worthwhile to put a tremendous amount of money into a program of training individuals to help themselves in areas of great poverty and in the ghettos? Could you recommend the techniques to make this a worthwhile project?" What would be your response to him?

ROGERS: I would say, "Yes, I think so." This presents two very basic problems for which we have test-tube solutions. One is this matter of really facilitating more individual independence and responsibility. The other is the handling of social tensions between individuals and groups. We know quite a good deal about how to deal with both of these problems in a small way—that's why I call it a test-tube solution. There is no reason why these solutions couldn't be escalated into much more significant methodologies that would help us in many ways. There is very little public recognition of the depth of this problem of how to help people achieve genuine choosing behavior. There would probably be a lot of resistance to it, because a great many people don't want individuals to choose where they're going. They prefer to tell them where they're going. But on the matter of the social tensions that exist, I should think there would be public acceptance of that because we could well afford to spend a few million dollars on relieving social tensions, interracial tensions, and that kind of thing.

EVANS: In terms of problems of vital significance in our culture, would you say such a government program should be regarded as on a par with our programs dealing with the prevention of cancer or heart disease?

ROGERS: I would regard it as more important. I really think that we should start a Manhattan Project, just as they did to develop the atomic bomb, to resolve some of the psychological problems that exist in our culture. We've mentioned two projects that I feel are very important. It is frustrating because I feel that in this sense, the behavioral sciences that exist outside of academic circles are in the same position as the Wright brothers who got a plane six feet off the ground and flew it one hundred and twenty feet. The majority of the public didn't believe it, and anyway, it was a perfectly useless venture. We're in that same situation in regard to some of these issues we've just been talking about. As psychologists, as behavioral scientists, we know that there is some basic knowledge there. There is enough to start, just as there was in getting a plane off the ground. What is needed is an enormous effort to expand that knowledge, to utilize it more broadly. Yet, the public is not ready to believe that that's possible, and perhaps not ready to want it, as I mentioned in talking about responsible individual choice.

EVANS: That's a very powerful statement. I hope that your words are heeded.

ROGERS: I hope so, too.

EVANS: Let's consider the social tensions resulting from identity-crisis problems of such groups as blacks, Chicanos, and females. Erik Erikson (Evans, 1969a) pioneered the analyses of such identity crises and the late Gordon Allport, in my dialogue with him (Evans, 1971), observed that we've shifted from a period of preoccupation with guilt to an increasing preoccupation with identity. Why have these tensions concerning identity seemingly become so manifest recently? What resolution do you see for all these various identity movements—black, Chicano, Indian, female, homosexual, blue collar, etc.? We're obviously going to be at the point where every single individual as a member of one group or another will in turn feel such identity tensions and begin to demonstrate his concern about his particular group identity. How ultimately can these identity tensions be resolved?

ROGERS: I'm not quite sure what causes all those tensions, although I will comment on that in a moment. I do feel that tensions are all linked together by one common psychological motive. It seems to me that people all over the world, and people in all kinds of groups that have not previously been heard from, are saying very loudly, "I want to participate in the choices and decisions that affect my future. I'm not going to be left out or shoved around like an object or a computer card." This is a very vital unrest. To me, it is basically a very healthy trend, but one that can be also very upsetting to many, many people. I think that, in part, it is due to the instant information of our age, though that is certainly only one factor. I'm sure that there have been various blacks throughout history who felt that they deserved more of a place in society, more right to choose, and to do what they wanted to do; but their voices were drowned out in the local area, and no one would ever hear about it. Now, the moment something happens, it's known all over the country, and other groups take heart and they decide they want to have something to say about themselves, too. One group you didn't particularly mention is the student group against the faculty and public. They're saying, "We want to choose what we're going to learn." So there is that whole wave toward participation, and growing, as I say, partly out of much wider information, and also out of the fact that it takes a couple of centuries for a concept to really sink in. A concept like democracy says you're worth something in your own right and you have a right to an opinion and you have a right to influence what goes on. I think that is gradually sinking in to the point where the average man has come to believe that's true of him and that's quite different from the feeling that somebody is granting you a privilege to vote. It's become a philosophical issue rather than just a political one. As to the question of how some of these tensions may be dealt with, members of our staff have had quite a little experience with black-white encounter groups, and some have dealt with labor-management groups. A lot of us have dealt with student-faculty groups. I would be willing to summarize our experience by saying that if two warring groups, to use that rather strong term, who are feeling a good deal of tension concerning their identities are willing to walk into the same room together and are willing even to talk *at* each other, not necessarily even to talk *to* each other, this is a beginning. Then, if there is a skilled facilitator to encourage and draw out communication, I think we could practically guarantee that some improvement in the degree of communication would take place. If that group was willing to stick together for a period, not necessarily continuously, but for twenty to forty hours, I would almost guarantee that better communications, better understanding, and more acceptance of each other would arise in that room.

EVANS: However, some who have looked at this

type of approach raise another question. Say, after the twenty hours in this type of facilitative environment you describe, they return again to an environment where this type of mutual acceptance isn't present. Then what? How does one continue this type of interaction in an environment which does not necessarily encourage it?

ROGERS: There needs to be a lot of follow-up and, furthermore, it's a thing that would justify a mass approach. If you were dealing with many small groups from a very large group, then you could feel that might have some real impact on the communities.

EVANS: A second-stage flow of communication could then emerge?

ROGERS: That's right.

EVANS: You used a very interesting phrase that we passed by rather quickly. You used the phrase, "a skilled facilitator" rather than "group therapist" or "National Training Laboratory-trained small group expert." Are you saying that perhaps individuals like these skilled facilitators in communication can play this kind of role so that we're not limited to the usual type of professionals to perform this facilitative function?

ROGERS: Yes. We have plenty of experience in that because we've had a program here for four summers now, and have trained a great many good facilitators. I would say that the kind of skills that a facilitator needs are attitudes that are not limited to any one profession or any one discipline, and that you can find these skills in a housewife, or a teacher, or a psychologist, or a priest, or other persons. Such skills are definitely not limited to members of one profession. We've also had experience enough to know that people who are not particularly skilled but who possess some basic attitudes can be trained in relatively short intensive periods to become much more skillful as facilitators of communication.

EVANS: You may be familiar with a rather interesting police–community relations effort in Houston (Cleveland, 1971). Police and members of the community worked together in the kinds of encounters that you mentioned. Although the program did receive quite a bit of attention, some believe it was ultimately unsuccessful for the reason we were discussing a moment ago. There was no follow-up and reinforcement of the program after the participants returned to their original environments. The danger in starting programs like this may be that a lot of enthusiasm is generated, and then somehow no visible impact is apparent in the final analysis. So the whole movement for such programs loses credibility. What can be done about this?

ROGERS: You mentioned one thing that could be done: one should not start a program of that sort without developing adequate plans for follow-up, for getting that group together again, or for getting groups with whom they're associated together. All kinds of ingenuity need to be used in regard to careful follow-up. The other answer that I've already suggested is that if it's just one small group encounter, even a protracted one, the effects can easily die out. If there had been several hundred people in each category, it wouldn't have died out. Follow-up for several hundred people takes funds.

EVANS: Moving now to another area of discussion, one can observe how Freudian and psychoanalytic theory in general has gradually seeped into popular culture. But just as popular culture is now at the point where it's beginning to really utilize these insights, among professionals at least, more traditional psychoanalysis appears to be of declining interest. Why has there been this decline in the importance of psychoanalytic theory among professionals?

ROGERS: Let me give a very simple answer first, and then explain it a little more. First of all, I think that the significance and impact of all religions are declining. The Freudian point of view in practice has certainly deteriorated into a very narrow orthodoxy which could really be compared with fundamentalism. Freudians must adopt this creed or else; and that's just not compatible with our modern way of thinking. I certainly would want to make it clear that this narrow orthodox point of view was not characteristic of Freud himself. He was a person who kept changing his thinking and revising his concepts and doing all kinds of different things throughout his life. He was a very fluid kind of person. His followers, who attempted to preserve what he thought, turned it into a very dogmatic orthodoxy. My only surprise is that it didn't die out a great deal earlier. I feel that Freudian thinking was dead quite a while ago, and people are just beginning to realize that now. I'd also like to say that it's quite true that some modern psychoanalysts have tried very hard to update Freudian theory, and to introduce some new ideas and emphases. I regard this as a noble effort, but I think it's too little and too late. People seem to recognize that. I may sound very harsh in these statements, but I'm being mild compared to the criticism that I have heard of psychoanalysis from leading analysts themselves. The year I spent at the Center for Advanced Study in the Behavioral Sciences, there were three prominent analysts there, including Erik Erikson. I've also known Franz Alexander. I can't reveal confidences, so I wouldn't want to quote what they've said. The most devastating criticisms of psychoanalysis have come from people like that.

EVANS: Yet, as I suggested earlier, psychoanalysis is an increasing part of the currency of popular culture. For example, important humanists like Arthur Miller, as he indicated in our dialogue (Evans, 1969b), actually are afraid that this has done damage in the sense that it gears people to an almost unhealthy preoccupation with themselves and their motives. It may actually destroy spontaneity in human interaction. Do you agree with Mr. Miller on this point?

ROGERS: Yes, I do. I think that it really is a damaging cultural influence, as it gets spread more widely in an oversimplified form. I think Freud's view that man is by nature evil and that the id is a terrible force which, if released, would play havoc, could lead to damage. The thing that saddens me a little bit is that one of the very real deficiencies of many of the advocates of the Freudian point of view is that they have never been willing to initiate research or to encourage others to do research on their various concepts and practices. Because of that, Freudian psychology has really relied on essentially unsupported dogma, and I think the world gets a little weary of that after a while. That's another reason for its decline. One thing that isn't mentioned often, one of the most unfortunate things that ever happened in this country, is that Freudian theory was never taken into the universities. Bob Hutchins made a real effort to do that at Chicago. He wanted to bring in Franz Alexander, and unfortunately this was opposed by some of the more solid scientists. I can understand their point of view. If psychoanalysis had found a real foothold in universities, it wouldn't have been so necessary to set up their own institutes. They would have been supported by tenured positions, so that they would have been secure instead of insecure, as I feel they have been. They would have been exposed to both the criticism and the support that is part of university intellectual life. They would certainly have been exposed to people interested in doing research on their concepts. That could have made for a viable continuation of Freudian theory and practice. This absence of acceptance by the university puts them in the position of a child who feels rejected by his peers. Psychoanalysts have drawn more and more tightly together and organized more and more defensively, which, in the long run, defeats them.

EVANS: Incidentally, there seems to be a resurgence of interest in Jungian theory. Do you think that this resurgence of interest and its greater focus on individual determinism is consistent with the overall interest in individual determinism as is reflected in your own views?

ROGERS: It might be. I'm reluctant to comment on that because I don't regard myself as a student of Jung's theories. Although I have said some things about Freudian theory, it's not in comparison with my own theory. I don't like to compare my theories with other theories because I feel that the person has a right to speak for himself and to be evaluated on his own. When people try to describe my theories, I find I don't even recognize them.

EVANS: If you sat in on some of the graduate seminars where Rogerian theory was being discussed, I guess you would be a little surprised at what you heard, wouldn't you?

ROGERS: I'm sure I would. But to get back to my assessments of the theories of others, a friend of mine summed it up nicely. This is an exaggerated statement, but there's a large element of truth in it. People who write, don't read, and people who read, don't write. I think that if I were to mention some of the people I have known that have the most scholarly knowledge and then if you should ask me what they have produced, it wouldn't be very much. On the other hand, people who produce don't have as much time to read. That may be partly a rationalization on my part, but I do not regard myself as a scholar in regard to many facets of psychological thinking such as Jung's, so I hope you perceive my comments in this light.

EVANS: You might be interested that, in my dialogue with Jean Piaget (Evans, 1973), he said exactly the same thing. It's possible that a lot of us do not have time to read the works of others as much as we would like. But it seems it would be a great disappointment to highly creative and productive people that other highly creative and productive people aren't really reading what they're doing.

Another object of criticism lately has been the use of the medical model in clinical psychology and psychiatry. A lot of this began with the rather controversial books and writings of psychiatrist Thomas Szasz (1961). Dr. Szasz believes that the medical model of illness and using such terms as *mental illness* are in themselves self-defeating and circular; that we've got to break away from this sort of thing that has created a myth of mental illness. How do you feel about that? Based on your own experience, would you agree with Szasz's position?

ROGERS: I don't know whether it's quite true that mental illness is a myth, but there certainly is a great deal of mythology about it. I heartily agree with Szasz in his belief that the medical model is totally unsuited to consideration of psychotic states. I want to continue to be open-minded. Some hereditary genetic factors which enter into the development of certain psychoses may be found. They may also be able to pin down definite psychological circumstances in which the person grew up. I believe that it is not satisfactorily dealt with in the doctor-patient relationship. In my several years of working with schizophrenics in Madison, I just came more and more deeply to believe that these are persons. One minor fact, which greatly interested all of us working on that project, emerged when we saw these psychotic individuals on a one-to-one therapy basis. Even though some of them were very disturbed on the ward and doing all kinds of "crazy" things, very little psychotic behavior was evident in contacts with them. It was very astonishing, because when you sat down and listened to this person and were eager to get whatever meaning he was trying to communicate to you, he communicated meaningfully. In times of great stress, he might escape into psychotic behavior, but the small degree of that was really astonishing to all of us. At this time I might tell you a story about an individual. There is one man who is quite fresh in my mind at this moment because I've just had an eight-year follow-up on him. When I began working with him, he was twenty-eight years old, and by the time he got out of the hospital, he had been hospitalized for more than three years. He was a person of ordinary intelligence. The hospital diagnosis was schizophrenic reaction, simple type—whatever that means. To me, it really means very little. In fact, I didn't even know that was the diagnosis until after I finished working with him for at least a year and a half, usually twice a week, although he couldn't always manage that. I guess I'm a patient person because there were the most incredible chunks of silence. It was not at all unusual to have a fifteen-minute silence. In some of what you might loosely call interviews, he didn't say more than fifty words. Yet he kept coming back, so that I felt the relationship meant something to him and so I kept on. He was quite a troublesome character in the hospital. He was often confined, and I'd have to go up and see him in his confinement room. Incidentally, there's a tape of an interview with him that's on file in the American Association of Psychotherapists' tape library. I cut out a lot of the silences, but it shows a little of the interaction. As I gradually reached him—and I don't know how I reached him except that I liked him and he gradually came to like me—his bitterness, which was the main element in our first meeting, began to die away and little by little he began to realize that some of the problems were in him. How he despised himself. He would say, "I'm no good to anybody; I'd rather die; I wish I could die; I'm no good to myself." He was really a highly despairing person. He lived through that, and I think lived through it because he did experience something of the fact that I cared. He began to consider the possibility of leaving the hospital. His behavior was fascinating then, because he would go to a lot of trouble in preparation for leaving the hospital, then would defeat the whole thing by being so disturbed on the ward that they would have to confine him and he couldn't leave. Then that wasn't his fault. He went through that about three times before he, over a period of months, came to realize he was the one that was afraid of leaving. As he faced that, and got to the point of leaving the hospital, he told me, "I'm afraid I can't make it, Doc, I'm afraid I can't make it." And I said, "Well, if you go out, I'll be glad to see you on the outside. If you can't make it there and come back, I'll see you when you come back here. So, that's all I can say. The decision's up to you. If you can't make it and feel you can't make it, OK." So, shortly after that, he left the hospital. Well, he left gradually. He went to class and came back every night to the hospital. That was his first step out. Then he tried a part-time job and moved out. But it wasn't too long after that I left Madison. I thought he knew where I was going, but there was evidently a misunderstanding, and he really didn't know where I was.

Last week I had a long-distance call, which is usually a bad sign for me and means that somebody wants me to do something, and the voice over the phone said, "Hi, Doc, guess who this is?" It was this man. He said he had been trying to track me down, and he just wanted me to know that he was doing well and was still at the same job. He said that he just wanted to let me know that he was ornery, sassy, and a good liberal. It was just incredible to have that kind of contact. Now, was he schizophrenic? Oh, I don't know. He was a troubled person who was not able to cope with society, that was certain. The one thing that brought him out of it, I feel, was that we were able to form a close person-to-person relationship, and the fact that his feeling about that relationship has continued through eight years is really astonishing. It's even more interesting because, until the very last portion of our contacts together, he would never have openly and consciously admitted that our relationship meant anything to him. It was only by his behavior of continuing to come for interviews that he showed it had a meaning for him. So it's things like that that make me feel that if you can reach the psychotic in a real relationship, you've got a chance of bringing him out of his psychosis. I don't underrate the difficulty of reaching such a person as him because, for most individuals who have turned to psychosis as an escape, life has hurt them so much and so many times, and they've been so disappointed in all their personal relationships that they don't believe you. They don't believe you care; they don't believe you're interested; they won't let you reach them because you may hurt them again. We did learn in our research there how terribly hard it is to reach some of these people. I still feel that a close human relationship is far more significant than anything doctors with superior knowledge of a patient who is ill can think of doing. I just feel the medical model is ridiculous.

EVANS: We're still somewhat in the grip of the nosological or classification-of-diseases approach to mental illness, where we have classified four or five types of schizophrenia, and we distinguish between psychoses and neuroses, and so on. It becomes a little like the early Ingrid Bergman film where the psychiatrist follows the patient around for a couple of days, and finally says, "Aha, you're a schizophrenic!" The audience is led to believe that this has somehow solved the problem, when of course, this is merely a label. This gets back again to some other comments playwright Arthur Miller made in our dialogue (Evans, 1969b). He calls such labeling of people as neurotic, psychotic, schizophrenic, or what have you, "psychiatric gossip." He really thinks such labeling in itself is very destructive as it gets into the currency of our culture. Do you think there is something destructive in even encouraging the use of such labels?

ROGERS: Yes, I feel that they are destructive, primarily because they make pigeonholed objects out of human beings. If I say you're a paranoid, then you're quite naturally placed. I don't even have to think about you as a person. You belong in that pigeonhole. I've been very interested to see this at work among psychiatrists. If one psychiatrist doesn't like another psychiatrist, then he begins to label him, calls him a manic, or says that he's got paranoid tendencies, or that he's essentially a schizophrenic. They're quite deceptive in that they're really finding a different way of saying they don't like that guy. They have to admit there's some truth in that. Now, I think it's a pseudothing; I hate pseudothings. They make it sound as though, "I know what illness you've got." Physicians overuse labeling, even in physiological diseases; but there are real diseases which they can identify and which deserve a label. To my way of thinking, in psychological states, there are certain patterns. Sure, there are people who are suspicious, and I would call them that instead of giving them a highfalutin label like paranoid. At any rate, labels give a pseudoscientific sound to what is actually a very loose and unfounded categorization.

EVANS: Of course, the thing that you are suggesting here is that our whole procedure of diagnoses of mental disorders may be rather faulty, because most of them really end up by being nothing but nonclarifying pigeonholes. In fact, a number of our psychological personality tests are really more or less designed just to place labels on people. Would you say, therefore, that maybe we are reaching a point where we should consider eliminating the use of many of our diagnostic personality tests?

ROGERS: No, I don't think we're just reaching that

point. I think we reached that point years and years ago. One of the earliest controversies in which I was involved was in regard to diagnosis. I felt that if you took the twenty or thirty hours that it usually took to get a "good" diagnostic procedure, and spent it on trying to reach that individual as a person, and tried to start therapy with him, you'd be several months ahead of yourself. I just feel that the use of diagnostic tests is worse than a waste of time. It is destructive and again puts the individual off in an object category where you can comfortably think about him without regarding him as a real person in a relationship.

EVANS: How deeply instilled is this old classification model in our various mental treatment facilities? Is it so deeply instilled that to break away from this will be almost impossible in the immediate future? Do you think there is some evidence that perhaps we can "crack" this kind of classification wall, which is actually a deterrent to helping people?

ROGERS: The reason I don't know quite how to answer that is that it is in one of your own fields of research in which you have published a book (Evans, 1968), the area of resistance to innovation. You know the resistance to innovation which exists in any setting. Such classification becomes ridiculous if the professional has been involved in one of those psychiatric or psychological institutions and has been involved in that whole rigamarole of diagnoses and so forth. If he sets himself up in private practice, he almost never goes through all that. He takes a person as he comes in and begins to deal with the person on a treatment basis, which shows that he doesn't believe at all in a lot of this folderol he's been sponsoring in the institution. As I see it, rigid classification has no logical or helpful basis. It has just become established as the custom or the tradition, and I wish tradition weren't so hard to change.

EVANS: To go a step further, there's a growing movement toward redefining psychiatry as *social* or community psychiatry. This movement, of course, is led by individuals such as Maxwell Jones (1952), Joshua Bierer (Evans and Bierer, 1969), and Marvin Opler (1959). They are all really saying that mental hospitals as we know them should perhaps be replaced by what they call a day hospital or turno (day-night) hospital. Even the so-called psychotic patient, instead of being hospitalized, should be kept in his normal environment and receive treatment on an out-patient basis at a day hospital. The leaders of the social psychiatry movement believe even the idea of a "mental hospital" is destructive. One of the major points that the social psychiatrists make is that training a patient to become adapted to the unreal mental hospital environment may be counterproductive if he ever has to adapt once more to his normal environment, if he is allowed to leave the hospital.

ROGERS: Yes, I agree very heartily that the place of the mental institution is very dubious, indeed, and I think that most people could be handled on a community basis. I'm all in favor of that.

EVANS: So, in a sense, you support this whole movement, which, if it continues on this course, may lead to hospitalization for a fewer and fewer number of so-called mental patients?

ROGERS: Yes, to support the point you made in your question, I can cite our project in which I treated schizophrenics. We found that many of them are suffering as much from what other people as well as I call "hospitalitis," as from schizophrenia. When you've lived a half dozen years in an institution, that's your disease, not anything else. It also becomes a very convenient means of family rejection. Families can say, "Well, he was so bad we had to place him in a mental hospital." That absolves the family of responsibility and gives them a nice rationalization. I'm fully in favor of doing away with all but the most minimal institutional care.

EVANS: British psychiatrist, Joshua Bierer, who represents a fairly radical view with his particular approach, has gone so far as to say, in the book on which he and I collaborated (Evans and Bierer, 1969), that many members of society not in hospitals may be more potentially dangerous to self and others than people in hospitals. However, he does feel the "criminally insane" should be hospitalized.

ROGERS: I don't feel well informed on that topic, but my offhand reaction is that people who have violently attacked others probably do constitute a potential danger. I would be in favor of a criminal sentence, rather than placement in a mental hospital. That may seem like a regressive step, but in my mind it's not. It says that this individual, even though perhaps irrational, still has some responsibility for his behavior, and that society has the right to incarcerate him for a while. It would give him the advantage, which the state hospital person does not have, of knowing how long his sentence is. You would have to have facilities for psychiatric and psychological care in the prisons. One of the worst features of the state's hospital system is that people are condemned to an absolutely indeterminate sentence. They have no notion as to when they can get out, or whether they can get out. Their life is really in the grip of a group of people who are, by and large, no more competent to decide than the ordinary citizen.

EVANS: Moving to still another area, there are those who would argue that our society is now experiencing a serious conflict of basic values which relate to our moral and ethical system. They suggest that a large segment in our society is bound by an ethical system to transcendental values, transcendental morals such as the Ten Commandments. These are absolutes of right or wrong. At the other extreme is a system which postulates situational ethics, where right and wrong are relative to the situation. For example, some of the current sexologists, talking about sexual behavior, indicate that any form of sexual activity between consenting adults, which does no harm to other people, is ultimately not wrong. Some students of the problem of the so-called generation gap argue that maybe this is really the heart of it. Our young people are operating more and more in terms of situational ethics and the parents, the older generation, are operating in terms of these transcendental, fixed ethical systems. How do you feel about that?

ROGERS: I see that as raising two related issues—the situational ethics problem and the whole question of the generation gap. I'll talk about them a little bit separately and consider situational ethics first. I think that it is much harder to live in terms of trying to evaluate each situation as to what is right conduct in this situation—what makes sense, what would enhance me, what would actualize me, and what would un-actualize me by the experience? Such a personal evaluation would be good for people interpersonally as well, because I think man nearly is an incurably social creature, and doesn't really get long-term satisfaction out of doing something that would harm someone else. It's difficult to know, in the complexities of modern life, the best course of action. If I just try to weight all the factors in it, it's much harder to live by it. A situational ethic is far sounder in this modern world than some absolute ethic. You do give up the consolation of knowing that you are absolutely right in what you're doing. However, the absolutist can have this comfort because he's living up to the moral code that someone established and which he has adopted. I've tried to describe the valuing process of the mature person in a chapter in *Freedom to Learn* (Rogers, 1969). It is as we try to sense the enhancing or constricting elements of each experience that we can form our own sense of whether this is valuable, enhancing, satisfying, growing, or whether it's the reverse. Then, in the locus of evaluation, the answer to who's going to make the judgment on this is always within the person himself. That's a tough way to live, and it takes a good deal of maturity. To my way of thinking, it's the only conceivable kind of ethic in a world that's changing so rapidly that the absolutist's formulas in almost every sphere do tend to go by the board. Take the matter of sexual ethics—rules which made absolute sense a century ago simply do not make sense in the present-day world, and I think the young people are quite aware of that. This might be a good bridge into talking about the other problem you brought up. What about our young people and the generation gap? I feel I've been very fortunate in having a good deal of contact with young people, students and others, and my grandchildren, three of whom, as I previously mentioned, are now in college. I have a great confidence in our young people. I only wish that we had begun to listen to them a number of years ago. I think that if they had been listened to, we might have avoided some of the violent exchange that concerns me a great deal at the present time, because violence is not going to be the answer for any of our problems. Violence is the final response, for the most part, of frustrated individuals who have tried every other means of accomplishing their goals, of trying to get somebody to listen to them and to realize that they are responsible adults, which many of them are. I'm not talking about the extremists, really, but about the great bulk of young people whom I think are the most hopeful group in our culture. That's quite true; they have very largely discarded many of the values of the older generation. They've tended to set up a new and very tentative code of values of their own. There's one point that almost all the young people in our culture would agree on at the present time, and that is that they bitterly hate phoniness and hypocrisy in any form. They've been brought up on it from Madison Avenue TV ads to politicians. They really know hypocrisy from the year one, and they do not like it. If they stick to that value, it's going to make a tremendous change in our culture, because we really are based in large measure on hypocrisy. Another value that I think they hold is that they're for flexibility and against rigidity. This applies to institutions, to personal living, and in every aspect of life. This means that they're opposed to the rigidity of educational institutions, to the rigidity of industrial institutions, and to the rigidities of religion. They are looking for a more sensible way of meeting reality. It's very much to their credit that many of them are trying to live this new set of values. They are making and will make plenty of mistakes in doing that. Some of the communes and all kinds of things that are going on are an attempt to live in this new set of values. They'll probably make just as many mistakes as we have, but I think we could stand some new mistakes. The world has had plenty of the old ones.

EVANS: So you think that such experimentation or even making mistakes by our young people is actually a form of growth for them?

ROGERS: Yes, I just have a great deal of respect for them. I mentioned communes, and that brings to mind another value that they seem to hold. They are really seeking in all kinds of ways for closeness, intimacy, and interpersonal warmth in a society that has become so alienated and so impersonal, it's very sad. I think they represent a real revolution. We have permitted them to go into a violent revolution which could be disastrous for all of us concerned. The real revolution that they represent could be a very constructive thing, and

I believe we could reduce the violence if we would listen to them. I can't blame them for being frustrated. They were old enough to die in Vietnam in a war they didn't like and didn't have any part in promoting or initiating, but they were not considered old enough to have any participating part in the culture in which they lived. Well, that would frustrate me, and that's putting it mildly. I can understand why they feel rebellious. Among the institutions, youth has very little regard for the institution of marriage. They're trying all kinds of new experiments in the sexual realm—again, some of which would be quite a mistake—but they are moving toward some kind of new resolution to our present very unsatisfactory situation in regard to marriage and the family.

EVANS: In this respect, there are certain magical words or phrases that lead to an immediate public reaction out of which considerable political capital can be made. These include "violence," "pornography," and "drug abuse." The so-called older generation is preoccupied with the fact that the younger generation is going to damage itself by exposure to violence, drug abuse, and pornography. However, not all members of the older generation are merely alarmists. Many have a genuine concern for these younger people. They may overstate the actual effects of these things, but they are concerned. On the other side of this, the young people feel that even genuine concerns are, in fact, restrictions. How do you see this?

ROGERS: Let me comment first on pornography. I think the report of the President's Commission is that all laws against pornography ought to be abolished.

That makes real sense to me. I think that we're put in the same situation as we were in regard to Prohibition. The more you try to deny a thing which a number of people want, the more they will find ways around the law. If it's open, then it can sort of find itself a place. I don't think there's any evidence that pornography does really serious social damage. Drugs are another matter. There is a drug culture among adults, but we know the drugs we're taking, and we know a little bit more about their effects. Every day you see people cutting off their lives by smoking. You see people hurting their brain cells, and this would include me, through drinking. We don't get upset about that because those things are of long standing. We do get upset about illegal drugs, and with reason. I'm sure that perhaps many of them have side effects that we haven't yet learned about. Many of the young people are concerned about them, too. If we could take a more factual approach to drugs, encourage research, and give the straight facts to young people, I think they would act sensibly. As it is now, plenty of their use of drugs is rebellion against the prohibition and the scare tactics. I regard that as unfortunate. For example, take the experience of the Beatles, which I've known to be repeated a number of times among young people I know. At first they got high on drugs. Then they became somewhat disillusioned by drugs and turned to meditation and other things to get their peak experiences. I think that's a path that a number of young people are following. There is a tremendous belief among young people in transcendental things; that is, blowing your mind is more than a phrase. They really believe you can enter new worlds of experience, and as an adult, I would like to be open-minded on that. They may have something to teach us. At any rate, if we believed in them, if we trusted them, if we listened to them, they would act rationally or far more sensibly than some of them do at the present time. I just feel that it's an incredible thing to have high government officials ridiculing young people and holding them in real contempt. I don't think that they realize that they're not dealing with a submissive group of servants or some lower category of people. They're dealing with thoughtful, well-informed individuals, many of whom are much better informed than the adult generation, and who are not going to stand for that sort of treatment. The worst thing that could possibly happen in this country would be an open revolution of the young against the old. That would be terrible for all of us.

EVANS: We talked about drugs, about pornography, and the third concern is the depiction of violence in our literature and on television. Again, to be concerned about this has become a journalistic cliché and the usual Presidential Commission has been formed. How do you regard this problem? Do you think it may be more valid to be concerned about the depiction of violence than about pornography?

ROGERS: Yes, I think that it is. I'm interested in the fact that I dodged that part of your question when you raised it first—I think because I am deeply concerned and quite uncertain about many aspects of that. I don't pretend to have any real opinion about whether the depiction of violence on the screen really causes people to be violent. I'm not sure on that score at all. I am sure that we are turning many young people into violent individuals, and that I deplore. You couldn't have watched killings and shootings and bombings in North and South Vietnam without somehow observing a little bit of the contempt for human life that was contained in all that. Many of the men have brought this home. It seems that violence is growing as a trend in the culture. It may be, as one of the radicals has said, that violence is as American as apple pie. It has been a part of our history, but I hate to see it as part of present-day history. There again, I guess I can only deplore it, and don't know very much about what to do about violence itself. I think we do have the beginning tools of how to prevent violence if only we would use them. You wouldn't get young people becoming violent if they felt they were in real communication with people in power who had some part in the decisions that were made. I remember one quite interesting high-school situation where a faculty decided to deal with a very difficult minority situation by making it a much freer place to learn. One of the first things that happened was that the blacks formed the militant Black Society and the Black Student Union. The Brown Berets organized the Chicano students. The neighborhood was terribly disturbed about this because the students wore armbands, marched, and did different things. But as the school brought the leaders of these movements into the school councils, and they helped to decide what should be done and what rules should be established, they became less and less militant in their whole approach to things. I feel that this is what we should do to really respect these people and bring them in on decision making, which then makes violence pointless.

EVANS: There is one final question that we might very well have started out with, which might have been a way of incorporating just about everything we've been discussing. As I read your work, and have over time been in contact with you, hearing you lecture, engaging in discussions with you, and so on, I have wondered what men and ideas have really influenced you the most.

ROGERS: I have no trouble in saying who influenced me the most, and the answer may be a little bit surprising. The individuals who influenced me the most are, first of all, my clients and the people I've worked with in groups. I feel that almost everything I've learned about personality, about interpersonal relationships, about personality dynamics came not from books or from some charismatic teacher, but from direct experience with the people I've been working with. Second would come the graduate students and other colleagues I've worked with. They've been a great stimulus to me. Now to try to answer it in a more conventional form, I would say I'm probably somewhat unusual in not having any outstanding mentor in my background. There's no one to whom I feel I have really looked up and said, "He's the one that got me on my way, and so on." I've had a number of people who've been stimulating, and who have given me new ideas, but there is certainly no one person. In this respect, I feel sorry for the people who have worked with me and are inclined to single me out as the major influence in their work.

EVANS: I'm puzzled why you feel sorry for individuals who state you have been a major influence on them.

ROGERS: That, I think, is, or can be, a little unhealthy. The students I'd be most happy to have influenced are those who have been willing to go beyond, who don't hesitate to differ with me, who are individuals in their own right. Sometimes in a group I'll come up against a person who says, "Oh, to be in your presence . . . This is just great because I've read everything you've written." You can just see the hero worship all over them. I like to tell people like that that there's a Zen thing that I really think is very fitting, and that saying is, "When you meet the Buddha, kill the Buddha." In other words, if you find the person who is the key to everything to you, this is the answer, this is my guru, etc., that's the time to wipe him out of that position.

EVANS: Do you really think growth stops at that point?

ROGERS: I do, I really do.

EVANS: That's very interesting. Earlier in our discussion, you suggested that the formal existentialist schools did not influence you directly, at least early in your career. What are some of the ideas that influenced you even from the beginning?

ROGERS: Well, I think I can trace some of the ideas that have influenced me. Certainly the ideas of John Dewey influenced me. I never worked directly with him, but I did work with his ardent follower, Kilpatrick.

EVANS: Among their contributions, Dewey (1971) and Kilpatrick (1933) were noted for criticizing the traditional educational system for its unwillingness to be sufficiently student-centered.

ROGERS: Yes. There's no doubt that a lot of my ideas about education couldn't be claimed to be original. You can hold an idea as an original thought of your own and yet be perfectly willing to admit that it's undoubtedly influenced by something in your past. That's the way I feel about my ideas about education. I have mentioned the later influence of men like Kierkegaard and Buber; I've really gotten a great deal out of that. I was fortunate in being able to hold a dialogue with Buber at one time. It was very meaningful to both of us. I can't pin this down to any one person, but I surely have been influenced by the notion of the whole scientific model, the hypothesis building, testing of hypotheses, and so on. I think that aspect has been very important in my life, even though at the present time I feel somewhat ready to leave this type of science behind. I don't want to give up any of the careful operationism, but it's time we developed a new kind of human science which will probably be quite different from the empirical studies we've made in the past. The scientific model has influenced me a lot. That's one reason why I was very fascinated to deal with the Cal Tech scientists and see scientists in quite a different field approach their work. Those are three trains of thought that I know have influenced me.

EVANS: Over the years you seem to have introduced some very complex humanistic concepts into psychotherapy. Yet you were almost alone among the psychotherapeutic theorists of the 1940s in trying to maintain a scientific stance in testing your theories. You formulated a series of hypotheses concerning the psychotherapeutic process which you seriously proceeded to test, unlike the nonobjective approaches characteristic of most other schools of psychotherapy.

ROGERS: That's true.

EVANS: Looking back at your work, even as you're still so active, what do you perceive as your most important contribution?

ROGERS: One thing that comes to mind at once that often has amazed me is that I seem to have enunciated principles in regard to interpersonal relationships that have been useful to an incredibly wide spectrum of different groups. That must mean something. It means something to me to know that business executives read my stuff, educators at all levels, psychiatrists, psychologists, social workers, priests and ministers. The range of impact that my work has had is fantastic. I stand in awe of that myself, and the only thing I can attribute it to is that they seem to feel that I have voiced some principles, if you will, of interpersonal relationships, of the way to promote growth and development in people in any situation, which they've found useful in a very wide variety of professional groups. I suppose one other contribution that I've made is a very simple one in one way, but I think it's had quite a wide influence, and it is the fact that I have been willing to pay attention to the raw data of interpersonal relationships: recorded interviews, all that kind of thing. It has given courage to some others to stop dealing only in abstractions, and to really get down to the basic raw data, and then to begin to theorize and build from that. I guess something I take some pride in is that I always wanted to get close to the raw data. I've not been a person who lives happily in a completely abstract world. I suppose related to this fact are my efforts to which you referred earlier, to make objective studies of very subjective phenomena. When I first came into the field of psychology, the thought that anyone could study a thing like empathy or congruence, or anything of that sort, would have seemed utterly ridiculous. Just as I mentioned earlier, I felt it was ridiculous to try to study the self. I didn't think it could be done. Then they were able to do it. So that, I think, has been a contribution that may point a little way in the direction of this philosophy of science that I hoped would emerge.

EVANS: Like any other innovator, in your own professional lifetime you have been the object of criticism, as you are aware. What kind of criticism was the most disturbing to you? What are some of your reactions to this criticism?

ROGERS: I'm pretty good at living and let live, so that the fact that people have held different points of view from mine has never troubled me much. Criticism that comes from honest viewpoints which differ quite sharply from mine are OK with me. I suppose the kind of criticism that I've liked least is the notion, which used to be expressed in many ways over the course of years, that the client-centered approach was a pretty shallow approach. It might do for dealing with superficial problems, but it really had not much to do with the deeper problems of personality. That is just not true. This criticism has probably troubled me more than any other I can think of, because I don't think I am superficial. You can't do anything but laugh off the fact that a lot of criticism is based on a complete lack of understanding of what I've been doing and what my associates have been doing.

EVANS: Concerning this same subject of criticism, the classic confrontations in the recent history of psychology have been your debates with B. F. Skinner (e.g., Rogers and Skinner, 1956). Thinking back to some of your debates with Skinner, I guess a lot was wrapped up in this whole issue of the control of man, where Skinner's point of view seems to support control of behavior toward a constructive end. Skinner suggests that if constructive forces don't control behavior, less constructive forces will and, in fact, do. Of course, these few remarks don't do justice to Dr. Skinner's views. But even his recent book, *Beyond Freedom and Dignity* (1971), may have been partly a reaction to your pleas for freedom and dignity in your debates with him.

ROGERS: Let me first comment on the personal aspect of it. Skinner is one of those whom I would certainly put in the category I mentioned a few moments ago—someone who holds a very different point of view, but whom I quite respect. He's honest about his point of view, and makes some attempt to understand my point of view. Our differences have always been sort of *clean,* if I may use that word. I mean we've been able to differ openly and yet without a lot of personal hostility. I suppose if there would be anything I would want to add to those debates, and this is kind of unfair with Skinner not here to reply, it would be that I think time is on my side. I'm sure he would feel just the opposite. I think there is an increasing emphasis in our culture, not necessarily in psychology, on the importance and significance of the person. Operant conditioning and Skinner's whole line of work has been a very real contribution, but I think that essentially time will show it to be a narrow contribution, in that we need something that includes much more of the whole person in the science of psychology.

EVANS: Direct offshoots of both your views and those of Skinner are prominent in the present Zeitgeist. Reflecting Skinner's views, behavior modification and behavior therapy are at one end of the spectrum as approaches to dealing with human problems, and those approaches are growing and proliferating at a fantastic rate. At the same time, the offshoots of your ideas in the whole personal growth, humanistic, encounter movement are also rapidly expanding. It seems to me that the one thing you and Skinner have in common is that you are both dealing with the contemporaneous problem of the individual. Neither one of the movements focuses on the past as psychoanalysis does. We are getting to the point where we are writing primers for the individual on how to shape and modify behavior, or come to grips with his true, humanistic inner being. Do you think that we know enough now in either of these approaches to hand a primer to a layman, show him a film or two, and provide insights that imply, "OK, now you, too, can do this"?

ROGERS: No, I don't think so. I'll just speak about what you call my end of it. I think that one reason I say no to your question is that the whole encounter-group movement is an experiential type of learning, and will never be fully captured within the covers of any book, primer or otherwise. The experience is something that might be pertinent for many, many people as they can enter the experience as quite naïve individuals, but I don't believe it ever will all be captured in a book.

EVANS: What about those who direct, supervise, and consult in the process of developing such groups? Do you think that we should maintain standards of minimum training or experience for them? As you know, establishing viable minimum standards for the psychotherapist has always been a real problem from the very beginning of psychology. In psychoanalysis everyone had to go through rigorous training, which included analysis of the prospective psychoanalyst. Do you think that we could almost allow anyone to begin practicing this "art" now?

ROGERS: No, I think that they do need training, but I think the training that they need is not typical or conventional training. It is more experiential. For four summers a program has been conducted by some of our staff members of this Center for the Study of the Person which trained individuals to be group facilitators. They don't demand too much in the way of paper credentials because they haven't found that to be of much help. It's more the attitude of the person that counts. The training they give is both cognitive and experiential. This is the kind of thing that is needed to prepare people to move into this field. As for setting up minimum standards, and so on, that's a very knotty question. I lean further and further away from that. I think all our attempts to set up minimal standards—I had a part in setting up the Board of Examiners in Professional Psychology and I'm not very proud of that—tend to freeze a given state of the art and science in a way that is not particularly helpful. It becomes a dead hand of the past where its whole intent is simply to protect the public. Even in the encounter-group movement, I know of no way of avoiding the risks that are involved in many people going into the field. I can only hope that the public will begin to discriminate between those who seem to provide helpful experiences and those who do not.

EVANS: Now, a final question: where do you go from here? What do you plan? What do you think you'd like to be doing in your professional activities?

ROGERS: I will introduce quite a personal note here. I find I'm not much good at planning my future. I *ooze* toward my future. That is one term I like to use because it reminds me of an amoeba that sends out these protoplasmic tentacles and then if it runs into something aversive, it draws back, but it flows in the direction that seems rewarding. And I feel that's the nature of my professional life. At the moment, my guess would be that perhaps I'm moving toward writing something that would be primarily for young people. I really feel there is so little attempt to communicate with the students, with other young people, but I would like to be able to do that in a humanistic, psychological way. I would like to try to write something that perhaps would deal with the problems they face in their lives as they see them, not as the adult world sees them. Now, that's a very euphoric kind of notion, and whether I'll be able to bring it off, I don't know. Beyond that, I want to get involved in many smaller projects, but that perhaps would be the only major one that I see coming over the horizon.

EVANS: Dr. Rogers, I certainly want to thank you for being involved in this project. I do appreciate your fine responses to often rather tough questions.

ROGERS: Yes, you've been pretty good at raising tough questions, but it has been enjoyable.

EVANS: Thank you.

PART VII

IN RETROSPECT: FORTY-SIX YEARS BY CARL ROGERS

IN RETROSPECT: FORTY-SIX YEARS*

CARL R. ROGERS

From 1927 to the present time I have been a practicing psychologist. I have made diagnostic studies of children and have developed recommendations for treatment of their problems; in 1928 I developed an inventory of the inner world of childhood which—may heaven forgive me—is still being sold by the thousands. I have counseled with parents, students, and other adults; I have carried on intensive psychotherapy with troubled individuals—normal, neurotic, and psychotic; I have engaged in and sponsored research in psychotherapy and personality change; I have formulated a rigorous theory of therapy. I have had forty years of "teaching experience," fostering learning through both cognitive and experiential

* This article was the Distinguished Professional Contribution Award address presented at the annual meeting of the American Psychological Association, Montreal, Canada, August 1973.

channels. I have engaged in facilitating personal development through the intensive group experience; I have tried to make clear the processes of both individual therapy and the group experience through recordings, demonstrations, and films; I have tried to communicate my experience through what now seem to me to be "countless" writings, tapes, and cassettes. I have played my part as a worker in professional associations of psychologists; I have had a continuous, varied, controversial, and richly rewarding professional life.

So it has occurred to me that there might be some interest in the question, What does such a psychologist think about as he looks back on close to a half century of study and work? It is to that question that I will address my remarks. What is my own current perspective on these years, thinking both about my professional life and its various periods of development and change?

An Astonishing Impact

I believe the major element of my reaction as I look back on my work and its reception is *surprise*. Had I been told, thirty-five or forty years ago, of the impact it would have, I would have been absolutely unbelieving. The work that I and my colleagues have done has altered or made a difference in widely different enterprises, of which I will mention several. It turned the field of counseling upside down. It opened psychotherapy to public scrutiny and research investigation.

It has made possible the empirical study of highly subjective phenomena. It has helped to bring some change in the methods of education at every level. It has been one of the factors bringing change in concepts of industrial (and even military) leadership, of social work practice, of nursing practice, and of religious work. It has been responsible for one of the major trends in the encounter-group movement. It has, in small ways at least, affected the philosophy of science. It is beginning to have some influence in interracial and intercultural relationships. It has even influenced students of theology and of philosophy.

My work has, to my knowledge, changed the life directions and purposes of individuals in France, Belgium, Holland, Norway, Japan, Australia, New Zealand, and South Africa; in twelve foreign countries readers can find some of my work in their own language; if someone wishes to read a complete collection of everything I have written, he will find it—in Japanese. I look with utter astonishment at this long list of statements.

A TENTATIVE EXPLANATION

Why has my work had such a pervasive impact? I certainly do not attribute it to any special genius of my own, and most assuredly not to any farsighted vision on my part. I give full credit to my younger colleagues throughout the years for their expansion and deepening of my thought and work, but even their efforts do not account for this far-reaching influence.

In a number of the fields I have mentioned, neither I nor my colleagues have ever worked, or been involved in any way, except through our writings.

To me, as I try to understand the phenomenon, it seems that without knowing it I had expressed an idea whose time had come. It is as though a pond had become utterly still, so that a pebble dropped into it sent ripples out farther and farther and farther, having an influence that could not be understood by looking at the pebble. Or, to use a chemical analogy, as though a liquid solution had become supersaturated, so that the addition of one tiny crystal initiated the formation of crystals throughout the whole mass.

What was that idea, that pebble, that crystal? It was the gradually formed and tested hypothesis that the individual has within himself vast resources for self-understanding, for altering his self-concept, his attitudes, and his self-directed behavior—and that these resources can be tapped if only a definable climate of facilitative psychological attitudes can be provided.

This hypothesis, so new and yet in a way so old, was not an armchair theory. It had grown out of a number of very down-to-earth steps.

First, I had learned through hard and frustrating experiences that simply to listen understandingly to a client and to attempt to convey that understanding were potent forces for individual therapeutic change.

Second, I and my colleagues realized that this empathic listening provided one of the least clouded windows into the workings of the human psyche, in all its complex mystery.

Third, from our observations we made only low-level inferences and formulated testable hypotheses. We might have chosen to draw high-level inferences and to have developed abstract, untestable, high-level theory, but I think my own earthly agricultural background deterred me from that. (Freudian thinkers chose this second course, and this marks, in my estimation, one of the most fundamental differences between their approach and the client-centered approach.)

Fourth, in testing our hypotheses, we uncovered findings regarding persons and relationships between persons. These findings and the theory that embraced them were continually changing as new discoveries emerged, and this process continues to the present day.

Fifth, because our findings have to do with basic aspects of the way in which the person's own capacities for change can be released and with the way in which relationships can foster or defeat such self-directed change, it was discovered that they had wide applicability.

Sixth, situations involving persons, change in the behavior of persons, and the effects of different qualities of interpersonal relationships exist in almost every human undertaking. Hence, others began realizing that perhaps the testable hypotheses of this approach might have almost universal application, or might be retested or reformulated for use in an almost infinite variety of human situations.

Such is my attempt to explain an awesome and otherwise incomprehensible spread of ideas which began with a very simple question, Can I, by carefully observing and evaluating my experience with my clients, learn to be more effective in helping them to resolve their problems of personal distress, self-defeating behavior, and destructive interpersonal relationships? Who could have guessed that the groping and tentative answers would spread so far?

PSYCHOLOGY'S AMBIVALENCE

You may have noticed an omission in the listing of the areas of impact of my work. I did not say that I and my colleagues have affected academic, or so-called scientific, psychology. This was not an oversight. I believe an accurate statement would be that we have had very little influence on academic psychology, in the lecture hall, the textbook, or the laboratory. There is some passing mention of my thinking, my theories, or my approach to therapy, but, by and large, I think I have been a painfully embarrassing phenomenon to the academic psychologist. *I do not fit*. Increasingly I have come to agree with that assessment. Let me amplify.

The science and profession of psychology have, I believe, profoundly ambivalent feelings about me and my work. I am seen—and here I must rely mostly on hearsay—as softheaded, unscientific, cultish, too easy on students, full of strange and upsetting enthusiasms about ephemeral things like the self, therapist attitudes, and encounter groups. I have defamed the most holy mysteries of the academic—the professorial lecture and the whole evaluation system—from the ABCs of course grades to the coveted hood of the doctor's degree. I can best be handled by most writers on psychology in one paragraph as the developer of a technique—the "nondirective technique." I am definitely not one of the ingroup of psychological academia.

The other side of the ambivalence is, however, even more striking. Psychology as a whole, science and profession together, has showered me with honors—many more, I believe, than I deserve. To my amazement I was awarded one of the first three awards for scientific contribution, and this was back in 1956 when I was much more controversial than I am at present. I had been chosen president of the American Association for Applied Psychology. I had been elected president of the American Psychological Association. I had been appointed or elected chairman of important committees and divisions, and these honors often touched me. Yet, never have I been so emotionally affected as I was by the scientific contribution award and its accompanying citation. When I was elected to an office, it could have been partly due to my ambition, for I was ambitious to get ahead in my profession. But this award was to me, in some sense, the "purest" recognition I had ever received. For years I had been struggling to objectify knowledge in a potential field of science that no one else seemed to be concerned about. It was not ambition or hope of any reward that pushed me on. In the empirical research itself there was more than a little desire to prove something to others—clearly not a scientific goal. But in the basic phases of the work—the careful observation, the recorded interviews, the hunches as to hypotheses, the development of crude theories—I was as close to being a true scientist as I ever hope to be. But it was clear, I thought, that my colleagues and I were just about the only ones who knew or cared. So my voice choked and the tears flowed when I was called forth, at the 1956 APA Convention, to receive, with Wolfgang Köhler and Kenneth Spence, the first of the awards for a *scientific* contribution to psychology. It was a vivid proof that psychologists were not only embarrassed by me, but were to some extent proud of me. It had a greater personal meaning than all the honors which have followed, including the first award for professional contribution, given last year.

I did enjoy last year's citation, especially the honesty of the statement that I was a "gadfly" to the profession—only now that statement promotes me to the status of "respected gadfly." I liked that expression of the ambivalence.

Two Struggles

As I look back over the years, I realize I have engaged in two struggles which have professional significance.

STRUGGLE WITH PSYCHIATRY

The first struggle has to do with the determination of many members of the psychiatric profession that psychologists should not be allowed to practice psychotherapy, nor to have administrative responsibility over "mental health" work, especially if this involved psychiatrists. I first met this opposition in Rochester, New York, when our highly successful Child Study Department, a branch of a social agency, was being reorganized in 1939 into a new and independent Rochester Guidance Center. A vigorous campaign, partly aboveboard and partly behind the scenes, was made to discontinue my services as director and to substitute a psychiatrist. There seemed to be no question about the quality of my work. The argument was simply based on the view that a psychologist could not head up a mental health operation—it was simply "not done." Although we had employed psychiatrists on a part-time basis for years, that suddenly became something that was out of the question. I could not point to any important precedent, nor could I claim the support of any professional group. It was a lonely battle. I am very grateful to the board of directors, who were almost all laymen, for eventually deciding the dispute in my favor. It had been a life-and-death struggle for me because it was the thing I was doing well and the work I very much wanted to continue.

After an interim lull at Ohio State University, the struggle was renewed with even more vigor at the University of Chicago. Not one of the rapid succession of chairmen of the Department of Psychiatry was willing to cooperate with the unorthodox fledgling Counseling Center. Finally, one of these men demanded of the university administration that the Counseling Center be closed, since its members were practicing medicine (namely, psychotherapy) without a license. There was still no professional support for our activities from the APA or any other psychological organization. I mounted a blistering counterattack, with all the evidence I could muster. Again I am grateful, this time to the chancellor of the university, for his (to me) fair-minded consideration and his suggestion to psychiatry that they drop their demand, which they did. These are the only two times I engaged in open combat with psychiatry. For the most part, my strategy has been twofold. I have endeavored to reconcile the two professions in their pursuit of a common goal. I have also tried to move ahead so rapidly and so far that the right of psychologists to practice in a field in which they were preeminent in research, and fully equal in practice and in theory building, could not be challenged.

But when pushed into a corner, as on these two occasions, I can fight with all the effectiveness that one develops in a family of six children. People who know only my thoughtful or gentle side are astonished at my attitude and behavior in a situation of all-out war. I should, in warning, have raised the banner of the early Colonies, on which was emblazoned a rattlesnake and the motto "Don't tread on me!"

I am happy to say that at the University of Wisconsin my joint appointment in psychology *and* psychiatry was a pleasant resolution of these struggles. Indeed, I initiated the formation of a group of psychologists and psychiatrists who gradually defused an incipient legal and legislative battle which was splitting the two professions in that state.

STRUGGLE WITH BEHAVIORISTIC PSYCHOLOGY

The other struggle of my professional life has been on the side of a humanistic approach to the study of human beings. The Rogers-Skinner debate of 1956 is one of the most reprinted writings in the psychological world. It would be absurd of me to try to review that continuing difference in any depth. I will simply make a few brief statements as I look back over these years.

To avoid misunderstanding, let me say immediately that I concur with the idea that the theory of operant conditioning, its development and its implementation, has been a creative achievement. It is a valuable tool in the promotion of certain types of learning. I do not denigrate the contribution it has made. But this is not the basis of divergence.

Let me also say that I have a great personal respect for Fred Skinner. He is an honest man, willing to carry his thinking through to its logical conclusions. Hence, we can differ sharply, without damaging my respect for him. I was invited by several periodicals to respond to *Beyond Freedom and Dignity* (Skinner, 1971) and declined primarily because I felt he had a right to his views. My one disappointment in regard to Skinner is his refusal to permit the nine-hour confrontation we held at the University of Minnesota in Duluth to be released. It was all taped and is the deepest exploration in existence of the issues between us. All of the other parties to the meeting had understood that it was agreed that the tapes, or transcripts of them, or both, would be released. After the meeting, Skinner refused his permission. I feel the profession was cheated.

I have come to realize that the basic difference between a behavioristic and a humanistic approach to human beings is a *philosophical* choice. This certainly can be discussed, but cannot possibly be settled by evidence. If one takes Skinner as of some years ago—and I believe this is his view today—then the environment, which is part of a causal sequence, is the sole determiner of the individual's behavior, which is thus again an unbreakable chain of cause and effect. All the things that I do, or that Skinner does, are simply inevitable results of our conditioning. As he has pointed out, man acts as he is forced to act, but as if he were not forced. Carried to its logical conclusion, this means, as John Calvin concluded earlier, that the universe was at some point wound up like a great clock and has been ticking off its inexorable way ever since. Thus, what we think are our decisions, choices, and values are all illusions. Skinner did not write his books because he had chosen to present his views, or to point to the kind of society he values, but simply because he was conditioned to make certain marks on paper. Amazingly to me, he admitted as much in one session in which we both participated.

My experience in therapy and in groups makes it impossible for me to deny the reality and significance of human choice. To me it is not an illusion that man is to some degree the architect of himself. I have presented evidence that the degree of self-understanding is perhaps the most important factor in predicting the individual's behavior. So for me the humanistic approach is the only possible one. It is for each person, however, to follow the pathway—behavioristic or humanistic—that he finds most congenial.

Saying that it is for the individual to decide is not

synonymous with saying that it makes no difference. Choosing the humanistic philosophy, for example, means that very different topics are chosen for research and different methods for validating discoveries. It means an approach to social change based on the human desire and potentiality for change, not on conditioning. It leads to a deeply democratic political philosophy rather than management by an elite. So the choice does have consequences.

To me it is entirely logical that a technologically oriented society, with its steady emphasis on a greater control of human behavior, should be enamored of a behavioristic approach. Likewise, academic psychology, with its unwavering insistence that "the intellect is all," has greatly preferred it over the humanistic approach. If the university psychologist accepted the latter view, he would have to admit that he is involved, as a subjective person, in his choice of research topics, in his evaluation of data, in his relationship to students, in his professional work. The comfortable cloak of "objectivity" would necessarily be dropped, exposing him as a vulnerable, imperfect, subjective being, thoroughly engaged, intellectually *and* emotionally, objectively *and* subjectively, in all his activities. This is understandably too threatening.

Let me simply add that what is really at issue is the confrontation of two paradoxes. If the extreme behaviorist position is true, then everything an individual does is essentially meaningless, since he is but an atom caught in a seamless chain of cause and effect. On the other hand, if the thoroughgoing humanistic position is true, then choice enters in, and this individual subjective choice has some influence on the cause-and-effect chain. Then, scientific research, which is based on a complete confidence in an unbroken chain of cause and effect, must be fundamentally modified. I, as well as others, have attempted partially to explain away this dilemma—my own attempt was in a paper entitled "Freedom and Commitment" (Rogers, 1964)—but I believe we must wait for the future to bring about the full reconciliation of these paradoxes.

In all candor I must say that I believe that the humanistic view will, in the long run, take precedence. I believe that we are, as a people, beginning to refuse to allow technology to dominate our lives. Our culture, increasingly based on the conquest of nature and the control of man, is in decline. Emerging through the ruins is the new person, highly aware, self-directing, an explorer of inner, perhaps more than outer, space, scornful of the conformity of institutions and the dogma of authority. He does not believe in being behaviorally shaped, or in shaping the behavior of others. He is most assuredly humanistic rather than technological. In my judgment he has a high probability of survival.

Yet, this belief of mine is open to one exception. If we permit one-man control, or a military take-over of our government—and it is obvious we have been (and are) perilously close to that—then another "scenario" would take place. A governmental-military-police-industrial complex would be more than happy to use scientific technology for military and industrial conquest and psychological technology for the control of human behavior. I am not being dramatic when I say that humanistic psychologists, emphasizing the essential freedom and dignity of the unique human person and his capacity for self-determination, would be among the first to be incarcerated by such a government.

But enough of this issue. I have strayed into the future. Let me return to my retrospective look and to some less serious reflections.

Two Puzzlements

There are two very different issues which have puzzled me; one of minor, the other of deeper concern.

REGARDING THEORY

By 1950, I wondered increasingly if my thinking could be put into a coherent theoretical form. At about this time came a request from Sigmund Koch (1959–1963) to contribute to his monumental series of volumes, *Psychology: A Study of a Science.* This was just the slight nudge I needed, and for the next three or four years I worked harder on this theoretical formulation than on anything I have written before or since. It is, in my estimation, the most rigorously stated theory of the process of *change* in personality and behavior which has yet been produced. As one young psychologist with a background in mathematics said to me recently, "It is so precise! I could restate it in mathematical terms." I must confess this is close to my opinion.

I was very pleased that it would be in Koch's series, because I felt sure that these volumes would be studied by graduate students and psychologists for years to come. I do not have exact data, but I suspect these volumes are in fact very little used. Certainly my chapter "A Theory of Therapy, Personality, and Interpersonal Relationships as Developed in the Client-Centered Framework" (Rogers, 1959) is the most thoroughly ignored of anything I have written. This does not particularly distress me, because I believe theories too often become dogma, but it has, over the years, perplexed me.

REGARDING CREATIVE LEADERSHIP

The second puzzlement is of a different order. In my younger years, while I was not a hero-worshiper, I definitely looked up to a number of men whom I felt were "*real* psychologists," whereas I existed on a poorly accepted fringe. I remember the community and professional furor when Leonard Carmichael was brought to the University of Rochester in 1936 as chairman of psychology: a special laboratory equipped to his specifications, a cluster of fellowships provided for his students, every acknowledgment paid to his brilliance and leadership. There was probably some envy in my attitude, as I labored away in a ramshackle frame building set aside for the Child Study Department of the Society for the Prevention of Cruelty to

Children, but my feeling was mostly one of admiration and expectancy. I felt the same way toward perhaps a half-dozen others—better trained in psychology than I, in my judgment more brilliant, with books and research studies already to their credit. Here were the men who would produce the great ideas in psychology, who would exert the same kind of intellectual and world leadership as that of outstanding chemists, physicists, and astronomers. I had no doubt at all that I had picked those who, a generation later, would be the preeminently creative and productive leaders of our science.

In every case I have been mistaken. Carmichael, since I have mentioned his name, has gone on to become a revered administrator, operating in the highest levels of the establishment. The others I selected have also had perfectly reputable careers, some outside of and some in psychology. But the dazzling promise of their younger years has not been fulfilled. For some reason this has puzzled me very deeply, because they have one attribute in common. They have lost any truly vital *creative* interest in psychology. Why? Were their interests too narrow and unsatisfying as they grew older? Did they lack any basic conviction or philosophy which might have guided their work? Did their efforts come to seem to them irrelevant to the larger social scene, their contributions too picayune? Was their initial work done primarily to impress their fellow psychologists, a motive which declines in importance with age? Did they endeavor to stand on and defend their early work, thus inhibiting themselves from reaching out into the creative unknown?

I do not know. It has thoroughly perplexed me and made me very wary indeed of trying to pick prospective leaders of creative thought.

The Sources of My Learnings

As I try to review all of the rich streams of thought and experience which have fed and are feeding my professional life, I can discriminate several of the most important sources.

CLIENTS AND PARTICIPANTS

First and overwhelmingly foremost are my clients in therapy and the persons with whom I have worked in groups. The gold mine of data that resides in interviews or group sessions staggers me. There is, first of all, the gut-level experience, which absorbs the statements, the feelings, and the gestures, providing its own complex type of learning, difficult to put into words. Then there is the listening to the interchanges in the tape recording. Here are the orderly sequences that were missed in the flow of the experience. Here, too, are the nuances of inflection, the half-formed sentences, the pauses, and the sighs, which were also partially missed. Then, if a transcript is laboriously produced, I have a microscope in which I can see, as I termed them in one paper, "the molecules of personality change." I know of no way of so combining the deepest experiential learning with the most highly abstract, cognitive, and theoretical learnings as the three steps I have mentioned: living the experience on a total basis; rehearing it on an experiential-cognitive basis; and studying it once more for every intellectual clue. As I said earlier, it is perhaps the most valuable and transparent window into the strange inner world of persons and relationships. I feel that if I subtracted from my work the learnings I have gained from deep relationships with clients and group participants, I would be nothing.

YOUNGER COLLEAGUES

The second most important source of stimulation for me is my symbiotic relationship with younger people. I do not understand this mutual attraction. I just feed upon it. In my youth I surely learned many things from my elders, and at times I have even learned from colleagues in my own age bracket, but certainly for the last thirty-five years any real learnings from professional sources have come from those who were younger. I feel a deep gratitude to all the graduate students, younger staff members, and inquiring youthful audiences who have educated and continue to educate me. I know that for many years, given the chance to associate with professional colleagues of my age or with a younger group, I inevitably drift to the latter. They seem less stuffy, less defensive, more open in their criticism, more creative in suggestion. I owe them so much. I started to write down examples, but to give a few would be unfair to the hundreds who have so freely contributed their ideas and their feelings in a relationship which has also lighted sparks of creative thinking in me. They have excited me, and I have excited them. It has, I hope, been a fair exchange, though I often feel I have gained more than I have given. I feel a great pity for those persons I know who are growing into old age without the continuing stimulation of younger minds and younger life-styles.

SCHOLARLY READING

Then much farther down the scale I would put what is often regarded as a major source of learning, the printed page. Reading, I fear, has most of its value for me in buttressing my views. I realize I am not a scholar, gaining my ideas from the writings of others. Occasionally, however, a book not only confirms me in what I am tentatively thinking, but lures me considerably further. Kierkegaard, Buber, and Polanyi, for example, would fall in that category. But I must confess that when I wish to be scholarly, serendipity plays a very important part. Serendipity, in case you have forgotten, is "the faculty of making fortunate and unexpected discoveries by accident." I have an eerie feeling that I have that faculty. Let me give you the latest examples. In preparing a current paper, The Emerging Person: A New Revolution, I was aware of a few of the writers who were presenting similar views. But then Fred and Anne Richards (1973) sent me a copy of their book *Homonovus,* just off the press. It was most timely. John D. Rockefeller III (1973) (I have had two contacts with him) likewise sent me a copy of his book *The Second American Revolution,* which was also highly pertinent. Then I was talking with a friend from northern California about my fantasies for my APA paper and he said, "Did you read the article by Joyce Carol Oates in the *Saturday Review?*" I had to confess complete ignorance not only of the article but of the author. His Xerox copy of the essay not only gave support to my view, but opened my eyes to a whole new facet of modern fiction. So, while one section of that paper may make it appear that I spent days or weeks researching in the library, at least half of that impression is due to serendipity. It has been a very frequent aid in my life.

My Concern with Communication

Still peering back—though my neck is getting stiff from that posture—I can see what is perhaps one overriding theme in my professional life. It is my caring about communication. From my very earliest years it has, for some reason, been a passionate concern of mine. I have been pained when I have seen others communicating past one another. I have wanted to communicate myself so that I could not be misunderstood. I have wanted to understand, as profoundly as possible, the communication of the other, be he a client or friend or family member. I have wanted to *be* understood. I have tried to facilitate clarity of communication between individuals of the most diverse points of view. I have worked for better communication between groups whose perceptions and experiences are poles apart: strangers, members of different cultures, representatives of different strata of society. To give adequate examples would compass the length of my career. I will cite only one. The filmed experience of a group involved in the drug scene included straight individuals, such as a narcotics agent, and "stoned" individuals, including a convicted drug pusher. There were blacks and whites, the young and middle-aged, ghetto products and members of the middle class. The group process by which communication and closeness became a living part of this diverse group is an experience I shall never forget. It is unfortunate that the film's title, *Because That's My Way,* chosen for us, catches so little of the vivid interchange which occurred (Station WQED, 1971).

This obsession with communication has had its own unexpected rewards. I held a half-hour interview with a young woman named Gloria (some of you may have seen the film) and a deeply communicative contact was established. To my complete surprise, she has kept in occasional touch with me for eight years, primarily in appreciation for the closeness we achieved. With Randy, the convicted drug pusher in the drug film, I was in constant correspondence for more than a year. Mr. Vac, one of my clients in our complex research on psychotherapy with schizophrenics, tracked me down after eight years with a "Hi, Doc," to let me know that he was still doing well and had never returned to the state hospital, even for a day. I think such rewards are savored more as the years go by.

In Sum

So I can sum up my informal look at my professional past by saying:

I am amazed at the impact of our work;

I have a dim comprehension that the time was ripening for it;

I look with amusement and affection at the ambivalence I have created in psychology;

I see with satisfaction the war with psychiatry concluding;

I am pleased to have played a part in the continuing drama of the behavioristic versus the humanistic philosophy;

I am puzzled and humbled by the disregard of what I see as my theoretical rigor;

I am perplexed by the later careers of some of the truly shining lights I have seen;

I am especially grateful for the gift of vital learnings from the people whose development and growth I have endeavored to facilitate;

I have confidence in the young, from whom I have continuously learned;

I discern more sharply the theme of my life as having been built around the desire for clarity of communication, with all its ramifying results.

The Now—and the Future

I should stop here, but I cannot. It is always a strain for me to look backward. It is still the present and the future which concern me most. I cannot close without a quick overview of my current interests and activities.

I am no longer actively engaged in individual therapy or empirical research. (I am finding that after one passes seventy, there are physical limitations on what one can do.) I continue to engage in encounter groups when I believe they might have significant social impact. For example, I am involved in a program for the humanizing of medical education. Up to the present, more than two hundred high-status medical educators have been involved in intensive group experiences which appear to be more successful in facilitating change than we had dared hope. Perhaps more humanly sensitive physicians will be the result. It certainly represents a new area of possible impact.

I have also helped to sponsor, and have taken some part in, interracial and intercultural groups, believing that better understanding between diverse groups is essential if our planet is to survive. The most difficult group was composed of citizens of Belfast, Northern Ireland. Represented in the group were militant and less militant Catholics, militant and less militant Protestants, and English. The film of that encounter portrays its difficult and partial progress toward better understanding—a first step on a long road. I see it as a small test-tube attempt which might be utilized in greater depth and much more widely.

I continue to write. I recognize that while my whole approach to persons and their relationships changes but slowly (and very little in its fundamentals), my interest in its applications has shifted markedly. No longer am I primarily interested in individual therapeutic learning, but in broader and broader social implications. Perhaps the titles of some of my recent papers (completed or in progress) will best give you a glimpse of where I am in my present work. The approximate titles are, "My Philosophy of Interpersonal Relationships and How It Grew"; "Bringing Together the Cognitive and the Affective-Experiential in Education"; "Some New Challenges to Psychology"; "Some Social Issues Which Concern Me"; The Emerging Person: A New Revolution. As I state these, the question arises in my mind, as it often has in the past, "Am I spreading myself too thin?" Only the judgment of others can answer that question at some future date.

And then I garden. Those mornings when I cannot find time to inspect my flowers, water the young shoots I am propagating, pull a few weeds, spray some destructive insects, and pour just the proper fertilizer on some budding plants, I feel cheated. My garden supplies the same intriguing question I have been trying to meet in all my professional life: What are the effective conditions for growth? But in my garden, though the frustrations are just as immediate, the results, whether success or failure, are more quickly evident. And when, through patient, intelligent, and undertanding care, I have provided the conditions that result in the production of a rare or glorious bloom, I feel the same kind of satisfaction that I have felt in the facilitation of growth in a person or in a group of persons.

REFERENCES

Koch, S. (ed.) *Psychology: A Study of a Science*. 6 vols. New York: McGraw-Hill, 1959–1963.

Richards, F., and Richards, A. C. *Homonovus: The New Man*. Boulder, Colo.: Shields Publishing Company, 1973.

Rockefeller, J. D., III. *The Second American Revolution: Some Personal Observations*. New York: Harper & Row, 1973.

Rogers, C. R. "A Theory of Therapy, Personality, and Interpersonal Relationships, as Developed in the Client-Centered

Framework." In S. Koch (ed.), *Psychology: A Study of a Science*. Vol. 3: *Formulations of the Person and the Social Context*. New York: McGraw-Hill, 1959.

Rogers, C. R. "Freedom and Commitment." *The Humanist*, 24(2), 1964, 37–40.

Rogers, C. R. The Emerging Person: A New Revolution. Unpublished manuscript, available from author, 1974.

Skinner, B. F. *Beyond Freedom and Dignity*. New York: Knopf, 1971.

Station WQED, Pittsburgh. *Because That's My Way*. (60-minute color film.) Lincoln, Nebr.: GPI Television Library, University of Nebraska, 1971.

THE EMERGING PERSON: A NEW REVOLUTION BY CARL ROGERS

PART VIII

THE EMERGING PERSON: A NEW REVOLUTION

CARL R. ROGERS

The Present Picture

That portion of Western culture which has developed in the United States appears to be in a process of decline and decay. Possibly the most important symptom of this is the growing belief of the people that they are unable to govern themselves—an increasing disbelief in the democratic process. Our cities are widely regarded by their citizens as ungovernable by elected officials. The rights and responsibilities of the citizen are no longer held precious. The Bill of Rights to our Constitution would almost certainly be defeated today if put to popular vote. Cynicism runs deep in regard to government and all its members. The distrust is reciprocated. Our government has a profound distrust of its citizens. There has been a steady drift toward a police state, in which force is the ultimate authority. As is clearly shown in the recent exposé of our federal power elite, the policy has been to use lies and deceit, criminal invasion of privacy, flouting of the law, the surveillance, harassment, and imprisonment of dissenters, to control the populace. Our foreign policy too indicates that we are but one step away from totalitarianism. It is dominated by the belief that "might makes right." In both undeclared and secret wars, bombing of defenseless peoples with no regard for their human or political rights is regarded as a suitable road to our diplomatic goal of so-called peace.

But it is not in government alone that we see the rot. Other institutions too are in decay. The churches ceased some time ago to have a significant societal influence. The family as an institution is in a state of disarray and confusion, with, in a great proportion of marriages, spouse alienated from spouse, and parent from adolescent.

As to the school, our public educational system is, by and large, ossified, failing to meet the needs of society. Innovation is stifled, and innovators squeezed out. In a rapidly changing world faculty members and their governing boards—whether local school boards or college trustees—tend to cling tenaciously to the past, making only token changes. It is probable that our schools are more damaging than helpful to personality development and are a negative influence on creative thinking. They are primarily institutions for incarcerating or taking care of the young, to keep them out of the adult world.

Economically, the picture is bizarre. The wealthiest nation in the world is said to be unable to afford proper health care for its people. The efforts to eliminate poverty are themselves being eliminated, while the top eight percent of the populace receives more income than the bottom fifty percent. This gap between the rich and poor in this country, and between the rich nations and poor nations in the world, grows steadily wider. Great corporations have an inordinate influence on our government and on our life, and even presumptuously interfere in the affairs of foreign countries. High office now goes preponderantly to men of wealth, so that of our one hundred senators, supposedly representing the people, forty are reported to be millionaires. The ordinary person has sensitive and compassionate representation neither in the corporation for which he works, nor in the government which rules him.

There are other signs of the times. As a people we lack any unified purpose, or perhaps any sure individual purposes at all. The alienation of youth from our culture is a matter of deep concern to many. The tendency of the individual and the group to use violent and criminal acts to serve all purposes, promote all causes, achieve all ends, is clearly evident. Here the people appear to be following the model set by the government.

So we have every reason to doubt whether our culture can survive. Sometimes it seems the only question is whether we will commit world suicide with the bomb, or simply decay until world leadership is taken over by other hands. It is not a pretty picture.

Some Brighter Views

But one lesson I have often learned in my garden is that the brown and rotting mess of this year's plant is a mulch in which next year's new shoots may be discovered. So too, I believe that in our decaying culture we see the dim outlines of new growth, of a new revolution, of a culture of a sharply different sort. I see that revolution as coming not in some great organized movement, not in a gun-carrying army with banners, not in manifestos and declarations, but through the emergence of a new kind of person, thrusting up through the dying, yellowing, putrefying leaves and stalks of our fading institutions.

More than four years ago I gave a very short, brash talk on "The Person of Tomorrow." I did not submit it for publication because I felt very unsure of my perceptions of this new person, and whether indeed he was emerging, or whether he was simply a wild fantasy of my own. But since that time my experience has only confirmed what seemed then to be a far-out thesis. Also, encouragingly for me, there has been a spate of books, from widely different sources, each from its own perspective seeing our culture undergoing some sort of drastic change, and producing a type of individual, a type of consciousness, a way of being and behaving, which will reshape our world. We have a solid medical scientist, Rene Dubos (1972), emphasizing that man's very makeup means that the future belongs to the "unique, unprecedented, and unrepeatable person," and that "trend is not destiny."

We have a poetic journalist-educator, George Leonard (1972), setting forth an almost ecstatic vision of the human species undertaking "an awesome journey into a higher state of being," a transformation he regards as inevitable. We have, from a very different vantage point, philanthropist-financier John D. Rockefeller III (1973) picturing the second American Revolution already in progress, caused partially by our much sharper and clearer awareness of ourselves and our world, and leading to a humanistic fulfillment of the American dream. A philosopher-psychologist, Thomas Hanna (1970), writes what is essentially a hymn to the wholeness of the pulsing, growing human soma—body and mind united—and to the new human mutants who are living that realization, leading us toward a new goal. A noted microbiologist, Jonas Salk (1972, 1973), leads us through his biological perspective to see an intellectual and spiritual evolution of man's unfolding potential. The Stanford Research Institute, through its social policy center, is about to issue an exhaustive report which asks how we may "facilitate the emergence of new images" of man, convinced that we must have a new and more adequate image if we are to survive. (Markley and staff, 1973) Two psychologist-educators, Fred and Anne Richards (1973), state the theme of their book in their one-word title, *Homonovus,* the new man. A far-out young medical researcher, Andrew Weil (1972), builds a case for this new man by pointing out the advantages of intuitive thinking—the natural mind—based on unconscious factors and altered states of consciousness, over the conventional rational thinking of the average man and the academic. Provocatively he points out that the future will belong to "stoned" rather than to "straight" thinking (though by "stoned" he does not imply drug-induced). A novelist, Joyce Carol Oates (1972) writes an essay about our "crisis of transition," where she sees the end of the Renaissance as man evolves into a "higher humanism." She uses what I regard as a marvelous quotation from Sir James Jeans, the physicist-philosopher. It expresses a theme which runs through all of the writers I have mentioned, who seem to be tolling the knell of a narrowly mechanistic view. Jeans says: ". . . the universe begins to look more like a great thought than like a great machine."

A New Configuration

I have given some snapshots of recent thinking about man as he will be—and other examples could be given. At any rate, such a diversity of strangely convergent perceptions of the future have emboldened me to present with more confidence—and with, I hope, more depth—my view of the radical new budding of persons which may change the fundamental nature of our society.

I should stress that what I will say is based on wide personal observation, on interactions with diverse individuals and groups, on my reading. It is an informal speculation, with all the possibility of bias and error that that phrase implies. It is not empirical science, nor is it intended to be, though I hope it may contain some elements of observation which will inspire further study.

It springs primarily from my experiences with what I have come to think of as new persons. Where have I found them? I find them among corporation executives who have given up the gray-flannel rat race, the lure of high salaries and stock options, to live a simpler life in a new way. I find them among long-haired young men and women who are defying most of the values of today's culture to form a counterculture. I find them among priests and nuns and ministers who have left behind the dogmas of their institutions to live in a way that has more meaning. I find them among women who are vigorously rising above the limitations which society has placed on their personhood. I find them among blacks and Chicanos and other minority members who are pushing out from generations of passivity into an assertive, positive life. I find them among those who have experienced encounter groups, who are finding a place for feelings as well as thoughts in their lives. I find them among creative school dropouts who are thrusting into higher reaches than their sterile schooling permits. I realize too that I saw something of this person in my years as a psychotherapist, when clients were choosing a freer, richer, more self-directed kind of life for themselves. These are a few of the places in which I have glimpsed something of this emerging person.

Though the sources of my perceptions are incredibly diverse I find a certain unity in the individual I am perceiving. The configuration seems similar, even though there are many minor differences. He (or she) —I wish someone would provide us with a bisexual set of pronouns—presents a new face to the world, a pattern of person which has not, in my judgment, ever been seen before, except perhaps in rare individuals. I would like to mention a number of the qualities of this multifaceted person, beginning with two which seem to be most prominent and most significant.

DESIRE FOR AUTHENTICITY

I find this person first of all to have a deep concern for authenticity. He values communication as a means of telling it the way it is, with feelings, ideas, gestures, speech, and bodily movement all conveying the same message. He has been brought up in a climate of hypocrisy, deceit, and mixed messages, and he is sick to death of doublethink and double-talk. He knows the falsehoods and guile of Madison Avenue. He has heard consciously deceitful statements from "the highest official sources" in our government. He has observed the word *peace* used to mean *war,* and the phrase *law and order* used to mean *repression of dissent by illegal means.* He has listened to the double messages of his parents and his teachers. All of these add up to the admonition, "Don't watch what I am or what I do; listen to what I say." He rejects this hypocritical culture which he sees, and longs to establish interpersonal relations in which communications are real and complete, rather than phony or partial. He has made astonishing progress in this respect. He is open, for example, about his sexual relationships rather than leading a secretive or double life. He confronts parents, teachers, government officials with his views, rather than giving a false impression of agreement. He is learning to handle conflict, even in organizations, and how to carry on continuing relationships in a climate of trust built on openness, rather than on a basis of facade. He is "for real."

So we have a highly honored young man, in his commencement address to the Harvard Law School, telling the assembled faculty and parents that "You have told us repeatedly that trust and courage were standards to emulate. You have convinced us that equality and justice were inviolable concepts. You have taught us that authority should be guided by reason and tempered by fairness. *We have taken you seriously.*"

He goes on to tell how, accepting those principles, students have worked for civil rights, labored in rural and urban ghettos, called attention to the injustices of the war in Southeast Asia. "Now, for attempting to achieve the values which you have taught us to cherish, your response has been astounding," referring to harassment and violence against such young people. "When this type of violent repression replaces the search for reasonable alternatives Americans are allowing their most fundamental ideals to be compromised."[1] He is challenging our two-faced culture.

We have an equally high-ranking woman student informing the commencement audience at Mills College that she does not intend to bring children into this modern world—because it is not a fit place. Such candor is unprecedented.

We have a B-52 pilot refusing an order to fly further

1 Meldon Levine, Commencement Address to the Harvard Law School.

bombing missions over a neutral country, risking court-martial, and saying, "To act as I was acting and to claim the moral convictions I was claiming was the highest form of hypocrisy." He takes full personal responsibility for flying the missions, even though he was acting on orders relayed from his commander in chief.[2]

Such painful honesty, such willingness to confront, and the willingness to pay the price of such utterances are indications of the value this emerging person places on being authentic, even in situations where tactful generalities have always been the tradition.

INSTITUTIONS EXIST FOR PEOPLE

One of the deepest antipathies of this individual is directed toward institutions. He is opposed to all highly structured, inflexible, bureaucratic institutions. He believes firmly that institutions exist for persons, and not the reverse.

One of the most striking cultural events of our time is the decline of the power and authority of the institution—in government, the military, the church, the corporation, the school. This is certainly due in part to the attitude of the new emerging person. He will not put up with order for order's sake, form for form's sake, rules for the sake of having rules. He questions every aspect of formal structure and discards it unless it serves a human purpose. He questions every inflexibility of any sort, with the belief that rigidity cannot serve the changing human being.

His beliefs on this score are not idle talk. He will

2 *Los Angeles Times,* July 28, 1973, p. 3.

leave an institution rather than give in to what to him are meaningless dictates. So faculty members drop out of universities, students out of colleges, doctors out of the AMA, priests out of their churches, executives out of corporations, Air Force pilots out of bombing groups. The list goes on and on.

Many of these actions are taken quietly, without fanfare. The institution of marriage is being deserted by thousands of couples, both young and middle-aged, who have chosen to ignore customs, ritual, and law, to live together as partners without the sanction of marriage. This is done openly, but without defiance. These couples simply believe that a partner relationship has significance only if it is a mutually enhancing, growing, relationship. It has, in their minds, little to do with marriage as a ceremony or as a legal step, and they simply disregard the traditional rules.

Or another instance of the attitude toward institutions is contained in a survey of Catholic wives. Of those under the age of thirty, over seventy-five percent are using methods of birth control of which the church disapproves. To the best of my knowledge there have been no demonstrations against the pope's 1968 encyclical. There is no wave of protest. These women are simply disregarding the institutional pronouncements and acting in ways that they see as best for persons, not for the structure. It is one more of the many instances which could be given.

What will take the place of the institution for this new person? It is too soon to say. One trend that I see is toward small, informal, nonhierarchical groups. Students and faculty have started five hundred "free schools," informal, often short-lived, decidedly unstructured, full of excitement and learning. A graduate school of high standards (Union Graduate School) permits a student to achieve a doctor's degree through an honest program of independent study by the student, advised and aided by a group of his faculty and peers. It is swamped by an incredible number of applications, and has attracted the highest type of true scholar, but it is keeping itself small. Business executives who have dropped out start personal enterprises limited in size, in which relationships are direct and face-to-face, rather than at second hand—or fifth hand. Persons of all types join communes, where the relationships are highly personal, and structure and authority are called into being only to accomplish a specific purpose. Some new professional groups, like the center to which I am privileged to belong, are primarily bound by a close sense of community, with no lasting lines of authority and no desire to expand in number, but carrying on diverse and creative projects in highly effective ways.

Another trend is to humanize the institution from inside, simply disregarding meaningless rules. Thus factory assembly-line workers disregard their assigned, routinized jobs, and form teams in which they trade off jobs, handle two jobs at a time, and in other ways pronounce, by their actions, that they are self-directing persons whose interests come first, not cogs in a great technological wheel.

In government and politics too—that quagmire in which so many men have sunk—some are endeavoring to take a human approach. Here is a successful state legislator writing to his constituents to say that "... institutions must become life-oriented rather than death-oriented ... That persons in politics be committed to ... self-realization rather than self-denial." He continues,

> Increasingly I come to realize that the discovery of a new politics for our culture depends upon my living and experiencing and discovering a "new politics" within myself—getting so much in touch with all the parts of my own being that out of the resultant oneness within me, I will increasingly live disclosingly so as to expose the institutions and customs of our culture which stand in the way of oneness—within ourselves, between ourselves, between us and the earth. (Vasconcellos, 1972.)

This is indeed a fresh breeze in the political world—an authentic *person* seeking electoral support, getting it, and changing a time-honored institution from the inside.

This second characteristic of the emerging individual—giving priority to the human person over the institution—is then highly pervasive, affects all organizations, and forecasts, in my judgment, a radical reevaluation of structure in our society.

Other Qualities

There are other qualities which I find in this emerging person. I will point to them briefly.

THE UNIMPORTANCE OF MATERIAL THINGS

He (she) has a fundamental indifference to material comforts and rewards. Though accustomed to an affluent society, and quite willing freely to use all kinds of machines, comforts, and luxuries, none of these is necessary to him. Blue jeans, a sleeping bag, and a hamburger are valued as much as—and sometimes more than—expensive clothing, fine lodging, and gourmet food. These material elements are entirely secondary to his main purpose. We find corporate executives who have become very comfortable as chicken farmers, or ski instructors, because they prefer those lives. We find young people with no interest in accumulating money, but only in using money for constructive personal or social uses. Money and material status symbols are no longer the primary goal of such persons.

A Nonmoralistic Caring

This person is a caring person. He has a deep desire to be of help to others, to his "brothers and sisters," and to society, when their need for help is clear. He is, however, definitely suspicious of the "helping professions," where "shrinks," social workers, and drug counselors earn their livelihood by offering help for pay, and too often hide behind a professional facade. He tends to take a more direct route. Young men and women man "hot lines" to aid those in crisis, and they do it voluntarily. They share food or lodging without question. When "straight people" are in emergency situations, they respond. In the floods along the Mississippi, long-haired young men and women rushed in, sometimes from hundreds of miles away, to fill sandbags, shore up levees, take care of families. And in all of this, financial compensation is a nonexistent or very minor consideration.

The help so freely given by this emerging person is a gentle, subtle, nonmoralistic caring. When a person is helped down from a bad drug trip, the touch is soft and supportive, without overtones of preaching. When an individual is caught in a crime, he is helped, not lectured or hassled. This person is acceptant of the individual in distress, with an awareness that the roles might easily be reversed. He flies in the face of the modes of "helping" most popular in our culture—the diagnostic, evaluative, interpretative, prescriptive, and sometimes punitive approaches.

THE WISH FOR INTIMACY

This person is seeking new forms of community, of closeness, of intimacy, or shared purpose. He is seeking new forms of communication in such a community—verbal and nonverbal, feelingful as well as intellectual. He recognizes that he will be living his transient life mostly in temporary relationships and that he must be able to establish closeness quickly. In his mobile world he does not live long in one community. He is not surrounded by family and relatives. He is a part of what Bennis and Slater (1968) call the "temporary society." So he realizes that if he is to live in a human context he must be able to establish an intimate, communicative, personal bond with others in a very short space of time. He must be able to leave these close relationships behind, without excessive conflict or mourning.

A SKEPTICISM ABOUT SCIENCE

One attitude held by this emerging person runs strongly counter to the prevailing view of the current and past decades. It is his deep distrust of a cognitively based science, and a technology which uses that science to conquer the world of nature and the world of people. He no longer trusts the abstractions of science, or the uses to which they are put. He has an intuitive belief that significant discoveries and learnings involve feelings. He is not especially thrilled by the space program, questioning the littering of space and of the moon with priceless "junk." He thinks that technology should exist for some purpose other than conquest.

One of the manifestations of his distrust of science as we have known it is his interest and belief in the occult, in astrology, in the *I-Ching*, and in tarot cards —the "sciences" of the past. But he has also been more than willing to engage in modern science and technology when he is convinced these serve human purposes. His expertise in electronics as a means of creating and transmitting music is obvious. His eagerness to use biofeedback as a means of enlarging his self-awareness, and to bring changes in his behavior, is another instance of this willingness.

His general distrust of scientific "progress" should not be misinterpreted. He is not dogmatic. He is eager to find truth. He is a searching person, without any neat answers. The only thing he is certain of is that he is uncertain. He is sharply aware of the fact that he is only a speck of life on a small blue and white planet (whose days may be numbered) floating in an enormous universe. He is, like many previous searchers, uncertain whether there is a purpose in this universe, or only the purpose he creates. He is willing to live with this anxious uncertainty as he, in his own way, strives to learn more of the two universes, outer and inner.

THE UNIVERSE WITHIN

For another characteristic of this person is his clear desire to explore inner space. He is more willing than previous man to be aware of himself, of his own feelings, of his "hang-ups." He is able to communicate with himself more freely, with less fear. The barriers of repression, which shut off so much of man from himself, are definitely lower in him than in preceding generations. He is a highly aware person.

This willingness to look within has led him into many new areas—drug-induced states of altered consciousness, a fresh interest in dreams, the use of a variety of types of meditation, a concern with all types of psychic phenomena, and interest in esoteric and transcendental religious views. He is convinced that within ourselves lie undiscovered worlds and hidden capacities—that daydreaming, fantasy, and intuition are but gateways to much more. To him cosmic consciousness, thought transmission, Kirlian auras given off by living things are not the ravings of "weirdos."

He regards them as within the bounds of possibility, and he is not afraid of upsetting a conventional world view by exploring them.

IN BALANCE WITH NATURE

This person feels a closeness to elemental nature. He has a respect for nature and its ways, and is relearning the lessons of ancient tribes on how to live in a balance of man's mutuality with nature, each sustaining the other. In his recreation, the surfboard, the ski, the sailboat, the glider are more symbolic of his interests than the speedboat, the dune buggy, or the racing car. The first cluster bases its excitement on a thrilling *alliance* with natural forces—waves, snow-covered slopes, the wind and its air currents; the second on the determined conquest of nature, with destruction and pollution as results. In his respect for nature this new person has rediscovered the value of patiently waiting upon the inhabitants of wilderness and desert in order to learn. We have men and women devoting long years of hardship to live with primitive tribes, or with gorillas, lions, chimpanzees, simply to learn from them. It is a new and respectful attitude, a more humble one.

A PROCESS PERSON

He is a person who is aware that he is continually in process—always changing. In this process he is spontaneous, vitally alive, willing to risk. His likes and dislikes, his joys and his sorrows are passionate and are passionately expressed. His adventuresomeness has an almost Elizabethan quality—*everything* is possible, *anything* can be tried.

Because he is in process himself, he simply will not tolerate fixity. He can see no reason why rigid schools, glaring maldistribution of wealth, depressed ghetto areas, unfair racial or sexual discrimination, unjust wars should remain unchanged. He expects to change these situations, and he wants to change them now, in human directions. I believe he is the first instance in history of man being fully aware that changingness is the one constant of life.

THE AUTHORITY WITHIN

This new person has a trust in his own experience and a profound distrust of all external authority. Neither pope nor judge nor scholar can convince him of anything which is not borne out by his own experience. So he often decides to obey those laws which he regards as sound and just, and to disobey those he sees as unsound and unjust, taking the consequences of his actions. On a minor issue, he smokes marijuana because he believes the law unreasonable and unfair, and risks being "busted." On major issues, he refuses to be drafted when he regards a war as reprehensible; he gives out "secret" government documents when he believes the people should know what has been going on; he refuses to reveal the sources of his news reports for the same reason. This is a new phenomenon. We have had a few Thoreaus but we have never had hundreds and thousands of people, young and old alike, willing to obey some laws and disobey others on the basis of their own personal moral judgment, and living with the consequences of their choice. He has a high regard for himself, and for his competence to discriminate in issues involving authority.

These are some of the characteristics I see in the emerging person. I am well aware that few individuals possess all of these characteristics, and I know that I am describing a small minority of the population as a whole. Yet these persons appear to me to be having an impact entirely out of proportion to their numbers, and this has, I believe, significance for the future.

Is This a Viable Person?

Certain questions may well be raised in regard to this emerging person. What is his chance of survival? What opposition does he, will he, meet? What will be his influence on our culture?

ANTECEDENTS

One line of thought which casts doubt upon his survival is a consideration of history. This emerging person bears little resemblance to the types of man who have shown survival qualities. He would not be congenial to the practical, disciplined, soldier-ruler produced by the Roman Empire. He bears little resemblance to the dichotomous medieval man—the man of faith and force, of monasteries and crusades. He is almost the antithesis of the Puritan man, with his strict beliefs and strong controls over behavior, who founded our country. He is very different from the person who brought about the Industrial Revolution, with his ambition, productivity, greed, and competitiveness. He is deeply opposed to the Communist culture with its controls on individual thought and behavior in the interest of the state. His characteristics and his behavior run strongly counter to the orthodoxies and dogmas of the major Western religions—Catholicism, Protestantism, and Judaism. He certainly does not fit into present-day culture—its government and military and management bureaucracies, its rigid education. He is not at home in our present American society, dominated as it is by computerized technology and the man in uniform—the military, the police, the intelligence agent, and the faceless men in control.

Is there any parallel? During the brief flowering of Greek culture it was believed that the highest aim of art and ultimate justification of the community was to create a *man*, a person of human excellence. The emerging person would be rather congenial to that goal. He would also, I believe, be more or less at home in the world of Renaissance man, during another painful and exciting period of transformation. But clearly his characteristics have not dominated past history. If he survives, he will be the exception and not the rule.

OPPOSITION

The emergence of this new person will be opposed. Let me suggest his opposition by a series of sloganistic statements which may communicate something of the sources of antagonism.

First, "The state above all." The past decade has given us ample evidence that in this country, as well as in a majority of others, the governing elite and the massive bureaucracy which surrounds them have no place for dissenters, or those with different values and goals. The new person has been and will be harassed, denied freedom of expression, accused of conspiracy, imprisoned for unwillingness to conform. It would take a massive—and unlikely—awakening of the American public to reverse this trend. Acceptance of diversity of values and life-styles and opinions is the heart of the democratic process, but it no longer flourishes well here. So this emerging person will certainly be repressed, if possible, by his government.

Second, "Tradition above all." The institutions of our society—educational, corporate, religious, familial—stand in direct opposition to anyone who defies tradition. Universities and local public schools are the institutions likely to be the most hostile to this person of tomorrow. He does not fit their tradition and he will be ostracized and ejected whenever possible. Corporations, in spite of their conservative image, are somewhat more responsive to public trends. Even so, they will be in opposition to the person who puts self-realization ahead of achievement, personal growth above salary or profit, cooperation with nature ahead of its conquest. The church is a less formidable opponent, and family and marital traditions are already in such a state of confusion that the antagonism, though existent, is not likely to be effectively implemented.

Third, "The intellect above all." The fact that this

emerging individual is attempting to be a whole person—body, mind, feelings, spirit, and psychic powers integrated—will be seen as one of his most presumptuous offenses. Not only science and academia, but government as well, are constructed on the assumption that cognitive reasoning is the *only* important function of man. One has only to read Halberstam's mind-boggling book to realize that it was the conviction of "the best and the brightest" that "sheer intelligence and rationality could answer and solve anything" (1972, p. 44). It was this belief that led us into the morass of Vietnam. This same conviction is held by scientists, faculty members, and policy makers at all levels. They will be the first to pour contempt and scorn on anyone who by word or deed challenges that credo.

Fourth, "Man should be shaped." As the Stanford report points out, a vision of man may logically be extrapolated from our present technological culture. It would involve the application of social and psychological technology to control nonconforming behavior in the interest of a regulated postindustrial society. Such controls would be exercised not by some one institutional force but by what the writers term the "warfare-welfare-industrial-communications-police bureaucracies (Markley and staff, 1973, xxi–xxii). It is clear that one of the first aims of this complex web, if this conforming image of man prevails, would be to control or eliminate the person I have been describing.

Not only may such shaping be brought about by subtle coercive control, but even by the steady advance of scientific knowledge itself. The biologist and biochemist are learning the possibilities of genetic shaping and of chemically induced alterations in behavior. These advances may, like social and psychological knowledge, be used as controlling or freeing potentialities. The physicists have long since lost their innocence in regard to the uses of their discoveries. The biological and psychological sciences are next. They too may easily become the tools of this massive bureaucratic complex in which movement toward control appears inevitable, with no one person responsible for any given step—a hydra-headed, creeping monster which would engulf the sort of person I have described.

Fifth, "The status quo forever." Change threatens, and its possibility creates frightened, angry people. They are found in their purest essence on the extreme right, but in all of us there is some fear of process, of change. So the vocal attacks on this new person will come from the highly conservative right, who are understandably terrified as they see their secure world dissolve, but they will receive much silent support from the whole population. Change is painful and uncertain. Who wants it? The answer is, *few*.

Sixth, "Our truth is *the* truth." The true believer is also the enemy of change, and he will be found on the left, on the right, and in the middle. He will not be able to tolerate a searching, uncertain, gentle person. Whether young or old, fanatic left wing or rigidly right wing, he must oppose this process individual who *searches* for truth. Such true believers *possess* the truth, and others must agree.

So, as this person of tomorrow continues to emerge into the light, he will find increasing resistance and hostility from these six important sources. They may very well overwhelm him.

What of the Future?

Yet, as history has shown many times, an emergent evolution is not easily stopped. This new person's arrival on the scene in greater numbers may be delayed by any one or all of the forces mentioned. The quiet revolution of which he is the essence may be slowed. He may be suppressed. He may have to exist only in an "underground." But a potent ferment has been let loose in the world by the qualities he exhibits. It will be difficult to put this genie back in the bottle. It will be doubly difficult because here is a person who *lives* his values. Such living of a new and divergent value system is the most revolutionary action a person can take, and it is not easily defeated.

Suppose then that he has an outside chance of coming into the light, of gaining influence, of changing our culture. What would the picture be? Is it as threatening or awful as many people might fear?

This emerging person would not bring utopia. He would make mistakes, be partially corrupted, go overboard in certain directions. But he would foster a culture which would emphasize certain trends, a culture which would be moving in these directions.

Toward a nondefensive openness in all interpersonal relationships—within the family, the working task force, the system of leadership.

Toward the exploration of self and the development of the richness of the total, individual, responsible human soma—mind and body.

Toward the prizing of the individual for what he *is,* regardless of sex, race, status, or material possessions.

Toward human-sized groupings in our communities, our educational facilities, our productive units.

Toward a close, respectful, balanced, reciprocal relationship to the natural world.

Toward the perception of material goods as rewarding only when they enhance the quality of personal living.

Toward a more even distribution of material goods.

Toward a society with minimal structure—human needs taking priority over any tentative structure which develops.

Toward leadership as a temporary, shifting function based on competence for meeting a specific social need.

Toward a more genuine and caring concern for those who need help.

Toward a human conception of science—in its creative phase, the testing of its hypotheses, the valuing of the humanness of its applications.

Toward creativity of all sorts—in thinking and exploring—in the areas of social relationships, the arts, social design, architecture, urban and regional planning, science.

To me these are not frightening trends but exciting ones. In spite of the darkness of the present, our culture may be on the verge of a great evolutionary-revolutionary leap. I simply say with all my heart: Power to the emerging person and the revolution he carries within.

PART IX

CARL ROGERS: CHRONOLOGICAL BIBLIOGRAPHY

CARL ROGERS: CHRONOLOGICAL BIBLIOGRAPHY, 1957 TO 1974*

1957

"A Note on the Nature of Man." *J. Counseling Psychol.*, *4*, 199–203.

"A Therapist's View of the Good Life." *The Humanist*, *17*, 291–300.

"Personal Thoughts on Teaching and Learning." *Merrill-Palmer Quarterly*, *3*, Summer, 241–243.

"The Necessary and Sufficient Conditions of Therapeutic Personality Change." *J. Consult. Psychol.*, *21*, 95–103.

"Training Individuals to Engage in the Therapeutic Process." In C. R. Strother (ed.), *Psychology and Mental Health*. Washington, D.C.: American Psychological Association, 76–92.

1958

"A Process Conception of Psychotherapy." *American Psychologist*, *13*, 142–149.

"The Characteristics of a Helping Relationship." *Personnel and Guidance J.*, *37*, 6–16.

1959

"A Tentative Scale for the Measurement of Process in Psychotherapy." In E. Rubinstein (ed.), *Research in Psychotherapy*. Washington, D.C.: American Psychological Association, 96–107.

"A Theory of Therapy, Personality, and Interpersonal Relationships as Developed in the Client-Centered Framework." In S. Koch (ed.), *Psychology: A Study of a Science*. Vol. 3: *Formulations of the Person and the Social Context*. New York: McGraw-Hill, 184–256.

"Comments on Cases." In S. Standal and R. Corsini (eds.), *Critical Incidents in Psychotherapy*. New York: Prentice-Hall.

"Lessons I Have Learned in Counseling with Individuals." In W. E. Dugan (ed.), *Modern School Practices, Series 3*,

* Publications from 1930 to 1957 are listed in *On Becoming a Person* (Boston: Houghton Mifflin, 1961), pp. 403–411.

Counseling Points of View. Minneapolis, Minn.: University of Minnesota Press, 14–26.

"Significant Learning: in Therapy and in Education." *Educational Leadership, 16,* 232–242.

"The Essence of Psychotherapy: A Client-Centered View." *Annals of Psychotherapy, 1,* 51–57.

"The Way to Do Is to Be." Review of Rollo May, *et al., Existence: A New Dimension in Psychiatry and Psychology. Contemporary Psychology, 4,* 196–198.

With G. Marian Kinget. *Psychotherapie en Menselyke Verhoudingen.* Utrecht: Uitgeveriji Het Spectrum, 302 pp.

With M. Lewis and J. Shlien. "Time-Limited, Client-Centered Psychotherapy: Two Cases." In A. Burton (ed.), *Case Studies in Counseling and Psychotherapy.* New York: Prentice-Hall, 309–352.

1960

A Therapist's View of Personal Goals. Pendle Hill Pamphlet #108. Wallingford, Pa., 30 pp.

"Dialogue Between Martin Buber and Carl Rogers." *Psychologia, 3*(4), 208–221.

"Significant Trends in the Client-Centered Orientation." In D. Brower and L. E. Abt (eds.), *Progress in Clinical Psychology.* Vol. 4. New York: Grune & Stratton, 208–221.

With A. Walker and R. Rablen. "Development of a Scale to Measure Process Changes in Psychotherapy." *J. Clinical Psychol., 16*(1), 79–85.

1961

"A Theory of Psychotherapy with Schizophrenics and a Proposal for Its Empirical Investigation." In J. G. Dawson, H. K. Stone, and N. P. Dellis (eds.), *Psychotherapy with Schizophrenics.* Baton Rouge, La.: Louisiana State University Press, 3–19.

On Becoming a Person. Boston: Houghton Mifflin, 420 pp. (Also in soft-cover Sentry Edition.)

Panel Presentation. "The Client-Centered Approach to Certain Questions Regarding Psychotherapy." *Annals of Psychotherapy, 2,* 51–53.

"The Loneliness of Contemporary Man, as Seen in 'The Case of Ellen West.'" *Annals of Psychotherapy, 2,* 22–27.

"The Place of the Person in the New World of the Behavioral Sciences." *Personnel and Guidance J.*, 39(6), 442–451.

"The Process Equation of Psychotherapy." *Amer. J. Psychotherapy*, 15(1), 27–45.

"Two Divergent Trends." In Rollo May (ed.), *Existential Psychology*. New York: Random House, 85–93.

"What We Know About Psychotherapy." *Pastoral Psychology*, 12, 31–38.

1962

"A Study of Psychotherapeutic Change in Schizophrenics and Normals: Design and Instrumentation." *Psychiatric Research Reports*, American Psychiatric Association, 15, 51–60.

"Comment" (on article by F. L. Vance). *J. Counseling Psychol.*, 9, 16–17.

"Niebuhr on the Nature of Man." In S. Doniger (ed.), *The Nature of Man*. New York: Harper and Bros., 55–71 (with discussion by B. M. Loomer, W. M. Horton, and H. Hofmann).

"Some Learnings from a Study of Psychotherapy with Schizophrenics." *Penn. Psychiatric Quarterly*, Summer, 3–15.

"The Therapeutic Relationship: Recent Theory and Research." Lecture given under sponsorship of the Los Angeles Society of Clinical Psychologists in Beverly Hills, California, January 19, 1962. Privately printed.

"The Interpersonal Relationship: The Core of Guidance." *Harvard Educational Review*, 32(4), 416–429.

"Toward Becoming a Fully Functioning Person." In A. W. Combs (ed.), *Perceiving, Behaving, Becoming, 1962 Yearbook*. Washington, D.C.: Association for Supervision and Curriculum Development, 21–33.

With G. Marian Kinget. *Psychothérapie et relations humaines: théorie et pratique de la thérapie non-directive*. Louvain, Belgium: Publications Universitaires, 319 pp.

1963

"Learning to Be Free." In S. M. Farber and R. H. Wilson (eds.), *Conflict and Creativity: Control of the Mind, Part 2*. New York: McGraw-Hill, 268–288.

"Learning to Be Free" (condensation of above). *NEA Journal*, March.

"Psychotherapy Today: Or, Where Do We Go from Here?" *Amer. J. Psychotherapy*, *17*(1), 5–16.

"The Actualizing Tendency in Relation to 'Motives' and to Consciousness." In Marshall Jones (ed.), *Nebraska Symposium on Motivation, 1963*. Lincoln, Nebr.: University of Nebraska Press, 1–24.

"The Concept of the Fully Functioning Person." *Psychotherapy: Theory, Research, and Practice*, *1*(1), 17–26.

1964

"Freedom and Commitment." *The Humanist*, *24* (2), 37–40.

"Toward a Modern Approach to Values: The Valuing Process in the Mature Person." *J. Abnorm. and Soc. Psychol.*, *68* (2), 160–167.

"Toward a Science of the Person." In T. W. Wann (ed.), *Behaviorism and Phenomenology: Contrasting Bases for Modern Psychology*. Chicago: University of Chicago Press, 109–140.

1965

"An Afternoon with Carl Rogers." *Explorations*, *3*, 104.

"A Humanistic Conception of Man." In Richard Farson (ed.), *Science and Human Affairs*. Palo Alto, Calif.: Science and Behavior Books, 18–31.

"Can We Meet the Need for Counselling? A Suggested Plan." *Marriage and Family*, *2*(5), 4–6. Queensland, Australia: National Marriage Guidance Council of Australia.

"Dealing with Psychological Tensions." *J. Applied Behavioral Science*, *1*, 6–24.

Foreword. In Harold Anderson, *Creativity in Childhood and Adolescence*. Palo Alto, Calif.: Science and Behavior Books, v–vii.

"Psychology and Teacher Training." In D. B. Gowan and Cynthia Richardson (eds.), *Five Fields and Teacher Education*. Ithaca, New York: Project One Publications, Cornell University Press, 56–91.

"Some Questions and Challenges Facing a Humanistic Psychology." *J. Humanistic Psychol.*, *5*, 105.

"The Therapeutic Relationship: Recent Theory and Research." *Australian J. of Psychol.*, *17*, 95–108.

1966

"Client-Centered Therapy." In S. Arieti (ed.), *Supplement to*

American Handbook of Psychiatry. Vol. 3. New York: Basic Books, Inc., 183–200.

Michael Polanyi and Carl Rogers: A Dialogue. San Diego State College and Western Behavioral Sciences Institute. 8-page pamphlet.

Paul Tillich and Carl Rogers: A Dialogue. Part I and Part II. San Diego State College. 23-page pamphlet.

"To Facilitate Learning." In M. Provus (ed.), *Innovations for Time to Teach*. Washington, D.C.: National Education Association, 4–19.

1967

"A Plan for Self-Directed Change in an Educational System." *Educational Leadership, 24*, 717–731.

Autobiography. In Edwin G. Boring and Gardner Lindzey (eds.), *A History of Psychology in Autobiography*. Vol. 4. New York: Appleton-Century-Crofts.

"Carl Rogers Speaks Out on Groups and the Lack of a Human Science: An Interview." *Psychology Today, 1*, 19–21, 62–66.

"Client-Centered Therapy." In A. M. Freedman and H. I. Kaplan (eds.), *Comprehensive Textbook of Psychiatry*. Baltimore, Md.: Williams and Wilkins, 1225–1228.

Person to Person (with Barry Stevens and Three Other Contributors). Box F, Moab, Utah: Real People Press.

"The Facilitation of Significant Learning." In L. Siegel (ed.), *Contemporary Theories of Instruction*. San Francisco: Chandler Publishing Co., 37–54.

"The Interpersonal Relationship in the Facilitation of Learning." In R. Leeper (ed.), *Humanizing Education*. Association for Supervision and Curriculum Development, National Education Association, 1967.

"The Process of the Basic Encounter Group." In J. F. T. Brugental (ed.), *The Challenges of Humanistic Psychology*. New York: McGraw-Hill, 261–278.

The Therapeutic Relationship and Its Impact: A Study of Psychotherapy with Schizophrenics. With E. T. Gendlin, D. J. Kiesler, and C. Truax. Madison, Wis.: University of Wisconsin Press, 625 pp.

"What Psychology Has to Offer to Teacher Education." In *Teacher Education and Mental Health*. Association for Student Teaching *1967 Yearbook*. Cedar Falls, Iowa: State College of Iowa, 37–57.

1968

"Interpersonal Relationships: USA 2000." *J. Applied Behavioral Science,* 4(3), 265–280.

Man and the Science of Man (edited with Wm. R. Coulson). Columbus, Ohio: Charles E. Merrill Publishing Co., 207 pp.

"To the Japanese Reader." Introduction to a series of 18 volumes of Rogers' work translated into Japanese. Tokyo: Iwasaki Shoten Press.

Review of J. Kavanaugh's book, *A Modern Priest Looks at His Outdated Church. Psychology Today,* p. 13.

"A Practical Plan for Educational Revolution." In Richard R. Goulet (ed.), *Educational Change: The Reality and the Promise.* (A report on the National Seminars on Innovation, Honolulu, Hawaii, July, 1967.) New York: Citation Press, 120–135.

1969

"Being in Relationship." Chapter in *Freedom to Learn: A View of What Education Might Become.* Columbus, Ohio: Charles E. Merrill Publishing Co.

Freedom to Learn: A View of What Education Might Become. Columbus, Ohio: Charles E. Merrill Publishing Co., 358 pp. (Available in hard or soft cover.)

"Graduate Education in Psychology: A Passionate Statement." Chapter in *Freedom to Learn: A View of What Education Might Become.* (See above.)

"Self-Directed Change for Educators: Experiments and Implications." In E. Morphet and David L. Jesser (eds.), *Preparing Educators to Meet Emerging Needs.* (Papers prepared for the Governors' Conference on Education for the Future, an eight-state project.) New York: Citation Press, Scholastic Magazine, Inc.

"The Group Comes of Age." *Psychology Today.* Del Mar, Calif.: CRM Books, Inc., 3.

"The Increasing Involvement of the Psychologist in Social Problems: Some Comments, Positive and Negative." *J. Applied Behavioral Science,* 5, 3–7.

"The Intensive Group Experience." Chapter in *Psychology Today: An Introduction.* Del Mar, Calif.: CRM Books, Inc., 539–555.

The Person of Tomorrow. Sonoma State College Pamphlet.

(Commencement address, Rohnert Park, California, June 1969.)

1970

Foreword and Chapters 9, 16, 22, 25, 26, 27. In J. T. Hart and T. M. Tomlinson (eds.), *New Directions in Client-Centered Therapy*. Boston: Houghton Mifflin. (All have been published elsewhere except the Foreword and Chapter 27, "Looking Back and Ahead: A Conversation with Carl Rogers," conducted by J. T. Hart.)

Carl Rogers on Encounter Groups. New York: Harper & Row, 168 pp. (Available in hard or soft cover.)

1971

Editorial. "Can Schools Grow Persons?" *Educational Leadership*, December.

"Forget You Are a Teacher. Carl Rogers Tells Why." *Instructor*. Dansville, N.Y. August/September, 65–66.

"Psychological Maladjustment *vs.* Continuing Growth." Chapter in *Developmental Psychology*. Del Mar, Calif.: CRM Books, Inc.

"Some Elements of Effective Interpersonal Communication." *Washington State Journal of Nursing*, May/June, 3–11.

1972

"A Research Program in Client-Centered Therapy." In Steven R. Brown and Donald J. Brenner (eds.), *Science, Psychology, and Communication: Essays Honoring William Stephenson*. New York: Teachers College Press, Teachers College, Columbia University, 312–324. (This paper, exclusive of the new Introduction [1971], was originally published in *Psychiatric Treatment, 21, Proceedings of the Association for Research in Nervous and Mental Disease*. Baltimore, Md.: Williams & Wilkins, 1953, 106–113.)

Becoming Partners: Marriage and Its Alternatives. New York: Delacorte, 243 pp.

Comment on Brown and Tedeschi's article. *J. Humanistic Psychol.*, *12*(1), 16–21.

"Introduction to My Experience in Encounter Group" by Haruko Tsuge, Dean of Women at Japan Women's University, Tokyo, Japan. *Voices*, *8*(2), Issue 28.

"Some Social Issues Which Concern Me." *J. Humanistic Psychol.*, *12*(2), 45–60.

"Bringing Together Ideas and Feelings in Learning." *Learning Today*, 5, 32–43.

Wood, John. "Carl Rogers Gardener." *Human Behavior*, 1, November/December, 16 ff.

1973

Comment on Pitt's article. *J. Humanistic Psychol.*, 13, 83–84.

Mousseau, Jacques. "Entretien avec Carl Rogers." *Psychologie*, 6, 57–65.

"My Philosophy of Interpersonal Relationships and How It Grew." *J. Humanistic Psychol.*, 13, 3–15.

"Some New Challenges." *American Psychology*, 28(5), 379–387.

"The Good Life as an Ever-Changing Process." Ninth of newspaper series *America and the Future of Man*, published by the Regents of the University of California, and distributed by Copley News Service.

"To Be Fully Alive." *Penney's Forum*, Spring/Summer, 3.

With B. Meador. "Client-Centered Therapy." Chapter 4 in R. Corsini (ed.), *Current Psychotherapies*. Itasca, Ill.: F. E. Peacock, 119–166.

1974

"Client-Centered Psychotherapy." Chapter for A. M. Freedman, H. I. Kaplan, B. J. Sadock (eds.), *Comprehensive Textbook of Psychiatry*. Baltimore, Md.: Williams & Wilkins.

Foreword. For translation of *Carl Rogers on Encounter Groups* in Japanese. In press.

Foreword. For translation of *Person to Person* in Japanese. In press.

Foreword. For French volume by Andre de Peretti about Rogers' work. In press.

With John K. Wood. "The Changing Theory of Client-Centered Therapy." Chapter in A. Burton (ed.), *Operational Theories of Personality*. In press.

"In Retrospect: Forty-six Years." *American Psychology*, 29(2), 115–123.

The Emerging Person: A New Revolution. In present volume.

Can Learning Encompass Both Ideas and Feelings? Unpublished.

Questions I Would Ask Myself if I Were a Teacher. Unpublished.

REFERENCES

Adler, Alfred. *Understanding Human Nature* (translated by W. B. Wolfe). New York: Greenberg, 1927.

Bennis, W. G., and Slater, P. E. *The Temporary Society*. New York: Harper & Row, 1968.

Bierer, Joshua, and Evans, Richard I. *Innovations in Social Psychiatry*. London: Avenue Publishing Company, 1969.

Buber, Martin. *The Knowledge of Man* (ed. Maurice Friedman). New York: Harper & Row, 1965.

Chickering, Arthur W. *Education and Identity*. San Francisco: Jossey-Bass, 1969.

Cleveland, Sidney E. "Psychological Intervention in a Community Crisis." In Henry E. Adams and William K. Boardman (eds.), *Advances in Experimental Clinical Psychology*. New York: Pergamon Press, 1971, 165–200.

Dewey, John. *The Child and the Curriculum and the School and Society*. Chicago: University of Chicago Press, 1971.

Dubos, Rene. *The God Within*. New York: Scribners, 1972.

Evans, Richard I. *Conversations with Carl Jung and Reactions from Ernest Jones*. New York: D. Van Nostrand, Inc., 1964.

———. *Dialogue with Erich Fromm*. New York: Harper, 1966a.

———. "A New Interdisciplinary Dimension in Graduate Psychological Research Training: Dentistry." *The American Psychologist, 21*(2), 1966b, 167–172.

———. *Resistance to Innovation in Higher Education*. San Francisco: Jossey-Bass, 1968.

———. *B. F. Skinner: The Man and His Ideas*. New York: E. P. Dutton & Co., Inc., 1968.

———. *Dialogue with Erik Erikson*. New York: E. P. Dutton & Co., Inc., 1969a.

———. *Psychology and Arthur Miller*. New York: E. P. Dutton & Co., Inc., 1969b.

———. *"Contributions to the History of Psychology: X Filmed Dialogues with Notable Contributors to Psychology" Psychological Reports*, 1969c, 25, 159–164.

———. *Gordon Allport: The Man and His Ideas*. New

York: E. P. Dutton & Co., Inc., 1971.

————. *Jean Piaget: The Man and His Ideas.* New York: E. P. Dutton & Co., Inc., 1973.

————. *Konrad Lorenz: The Man and His Ideas.* New York: Harcourt, Brace, Jovanovich, in press.

Freud, Sigmund. *The Standard Edition of the Complete Psychological Works of Sigmund Freud* (ed. James Stracher). London: The Hogarth Press, 1953–

Goldstein, Kurt. *The Organism.* New York: American Book Company, 1939.

Halberstam, David. *The Best and the Brightest.* New York: Random House, 1972.

Hanna, Thomas. *Bodies in Revolt.* New York: Holt, Rinehart & Winston, 1970.

Hayek, F. A. "The Dilemma of Specialization." In Leonard D. White (ed.), *The State of the Social Sciences.* Chicago: University of Chicago Press, 1956.

Heidegger, Martin. *An Introduction to Metaphysics* (translated by R. Manheim). New Haven, Conn.: Yale University Press, 1959.

Horney, Karen. *The Neurotic Personality of Our Time.* New York: W. W. Norton & Co., 1937.

Hull, C. L. *Principles of Behavior.* New York: Appleton, 1943.

Husserl, Edmund. *Ideas: General Introduction to Pure Phenomenology* (translated by W. R. Boyce Gibson). New York: The Macmillan Company, 1952.

Jones, Maxwell. *Social Psychiatry.* London: Tavistock Publications, 1952.

Kardiner, Abram. *The Individual and His Society.* New York: Columbia University Press, 1939.

Kenniston, Kenneth. "The Sources of Student Dissent." *Journal of Social Issues,* 25(3), 1967, 103–137.

Kilpatrick, William H. (ed.). *The Educational Frontier.* New York: The Century Company, 1933.

Lasswell, Harold. "Must Science Serve Political Power?" *American Psychology,* 25(2), 1970, 117–123.

Leonard, George B. *The Transformation: A Guide to the Inevitable Changes in Humankind.* New York: Delacorte, 1972.

McClelland, David C. *The Achievement Motive.* New York: Appleton-Century-Crofts, 1953.

McCurdy, Harold G. *The Personal World: An Introduction to*

the Study of Personality. New York: Appleton-Century-Crofts, 1953.

Markley, O. W., and staff. "Changing Images of Man." Report prepared for the Stanford Research Institute, first draft, 1973.

Maslow, Abraham H. *Motivation and Personality*. New York: Harper & Brothers, 1954.

May, Rollo. "Existential Basis of Psychotherapy." In Rollo May (ed.), *Existential Psychology*. New York: Random House, 1961.

Murray, Henry A., Barrett, William G., and Homburger, Erik. *Explorations in Personality*. New York: Oxford University Press, 1938.

Oates, Joyce Carol. "New Heaven and Earth." *Saturday Review*, November 4, 1972, 51–54.

Opler, Marvin K. (ed.). *Culture and Mental Health*. New York: The Macmillan Company, 1959.

Richards, Fred, and Richards, Anne C. *Homonovus: The New Man*. Boulder, Colo.: Shields Publishing Company, 1973.

Rockefeller, J. D., III. *The Second American Revolution*. New York: Harper & Row, 1973.

Rogers, Carl R., and Skinner, B. F. "Some Issues Concerning the Control of Human Behavior." *Science*, 124, 1956, 1057–1065.

Rogers, Carl R. *Freedom to Learn*. Columbus, Ohio: Charles E. Merrill Publishing Company, 1969.

———. *Carl Rogers on Encounter Groups*. New York: Harper & Row, 1970.

Salk, Jonas. *Man Unfolding*. New York: Harper & Row, 1972.

———. *The Survival of the Wisest*. New York: Harper & Row, 1973.

Sanford, Nevitt. *The American College*. New York: Wiley, 1962.

———. "Will Psychologists Study Human Problems?" *The American Psychologist*, 20(3), 1965, 192–202.

Skinner, B. F. *Beyond Freedom and Dignity*. New York: Knopf, 1971.

Stephenson, William. *The Study of Behavior: Q-Technique and Its Methodology*. Chicago: University of Chicago Press, 1953.

Sullivan, H. S. *The Interpersonal Theory of Psychiatry*. New York: W. W. Norton & Company, 1953.

Szasz, Thomas. *The Myth of Mental Illness.* New York: Hueber-Harper, 1961.

Tillich, Paul. *The Courage to Be.* New Haven, Conn.: Yale University Press, 1952.

Tolman, E. C. *Purposive Behavior in Animals and Men.* New York: Century, 1932.

Vasconcellos, J. Communication to Constituents. 1972.

Weil, Andrew. *The Natural Mind.* Boston: Houghton Mifflin Co., 1972.

INDEX

ABOUT THE AUTHOR

RICHARD I. EVANS received his Ph.D. from Michigan State University and is currently professor of psychology at the University of Houston. He is the Director of the Social Psychology/Behavioral Medicine Research and Graduate Training Group.

A National Science Foundation grant has enabled him to film discussions and complete books with some of the world's foremost behavioral scientists including the distinguished participants in the dialogues in this Praeger Series.

He is a pioneer in public television and in the social psychology of communication, and has published over a hundred articles in the area of social psychology. In addition to the volumes in this Dialogue Series, his books include *Social Psychology in Life* (with Richard Rozelle), *Resistance in Innovation in Higher Education, The Making of Psychology,* and *The Making of Social Psychology.*

His recent honors include the American Psychological Foundation Media Awards for the book, *Gordon Allport: The Man and His Ideas* and the film, "A Psychology of Creativity." He and his colleagues received American Psychological Association Division 13 Research Excellence Awards in 1970, 1973, and 1977 for their work in social psychology in behavioral medicine. He received the Phi Kappa Phi National Distinguished Scholar Award for the 1974-77 Triennium, and the 1980 Ester Farfel Award, the University of Houston's highest award for excellence in teaching, research and service.